WHEN THE LEVEE BREAKS

MEMPHIS AND THE MISSISSIPPI VALLEY FLOOD OF 1927

PATRICK O'DANIEL

Charleston | London

THE
History
PRESS

Published by The History Press
Charleston, SC 29403
www.historypress.net

First published 2013

Manufactured in the United States

ISBN 978.1.60949.942.6

Library of Congress CIP data applied for.

CONTENTS

Acknowledgements   5
Introduction   7

1. The Greatest on Record   11
2. When the Levee Breaks   19
3. Higher Ground   38
4. Water, Land and Air   49
5. Colossus of the Mississippi Flood Disaster   68
6. Good Samaritan City of the Mississippi   82
7. Politics of New Flood Control   108

Epilogue   117
Notes   119
Index   137
About the Author   144

ACKNOWLEDGEMENTS

I would like to thank the staff of the Memphis Room and the history/social sciences department of the Memphis Public Library and Information Center, the West Tennessee Historical Society, the University of Mississippi Archives and Special Collections, the University of Memphis Special Collections Department and the staff of The History Press for giving me the opportunity to publish this book. I would also like to thank all my friends and family for their love and support—especially Kathy and Kelly, to whom I dedicate this book.

INTRODUCTION

Oh, Lordy, women and grown men drown
Oh, women and children sinkin' down
Lord, have mercy
I couldn't see nobody's home and wasn't no one to be found
—Charley Patton, "High Water Everywhere, Part 2"[1]

The line of refugees stretched for miles along the road to Memphis. The mud-covered and bewildered people trudged along in trucks, horse-drawn carts or on foot toward the Harahan Bridge, which spanned the Mississippi River and connected the city to its neighbors in eastern Arkansas. Their levees on the western side of the river had broken during the night, and their homes, farms and towns were flooded. In a matter of hours, yellow river water covered everything they had known. It destroyed freshly planted fields, drowned livestock and killed neighbors and family. The long line of survivors marched to Memphis to escape the water and mosquitoes and the stench of mud, mold and rotting vegetation.

The bedraggled Arkansans had no idea what kind of reception Memphians would offer, but they certainly did not expect to meet the contingent of waiting police. With nothing but muck and mire behind them, the refugees had little choice but to follow the armed escort into Memphis. They would find sanctuary and charity in the city; however, they would find it within the confines of a guarded concentration camp.

Meanwhile, Memphians hastily organized mercy missions into Arkansas and Mississippi. They navigated the raging torrents of the river and flooded farmlands to rescue stranded flood victims and deliver food, medicine and news to the areas hardest hit. Even the most experienced rivermen had never seen devastation on the scale they found when they ventured into the muddy apocalypse left in the wake of the levee breaks.

The massive storm that struck the southern United States on April 15, 1927, caused the worst flood to strike the Mississippi Valley in recorded history. Heavy rains inundated large parts of Arkansas, Illinois, Kentucky, Louisiana, Mississippi, Missouri and Tennessee. Rivers spilled over their banks and crevassed the levees. Soon, the murky yellow water covered approximately twenty-seven thousand square miles, ruining crops, damaging or destroying 137,000 buildings, displacing 700,000 people and killing over 250 others. However, the misery did not end there. Unrepaired levees allowed subsequent high water to keep the affected areas flooded through the summer.

The Red Cross and the U.S. Weather Bureau estimated the direct economic losses along the lower Mississippi River between $250 and $350 million, with Louisiana and Arkansas taking the heaviest destruction out of all the states affected by the flood. To appreciate the extent of the devastation, one should consider a report that measured the damages at 2007 values.[2]

STATE	RESIDENTIAL DAMAGES	COMMERCIAL DAMAGES
Illinois	$0.2 billion	$0.1 billion
Kentucky	$0.3 billion	$0.5–$1.0 billion
Missouri	$6.5–$8.0 billion	$3.5–$5.0 billion
Mississippi	$8.0–$9.0 billion	$3.0–$4.0 billion
Tennessee	$9.5–$11.5 billion	$6.0–$7.5 billion
Arkansas	$30.0–$33.5 billion	$14.5–$18.5 billion
Louisiana	$37.0–$42.0 billion	$15.0–$21.0 billion

A *Time* magazine reporter described the disaster in the Mississippi Valley: "All around raged tragedy, havoc, cosmic comedy." President Calvin Coolidge appointed a special committee made up of his most trusted cabinet secretaries—Herbert Hoover, Andrew Mellon, Curtis Wilbur and Dwight Davis—to work with the Red Cross to organize relief efforts to help the flood victims. Relief workers rushed into the flood zone in the wake of the levee breaks, while state militia tried to maintain order and rescue teams worked to convince stubborn and panicky people to leave their homes and belongings to seek shelter in camps on higher ground.[3]

In the middle of the chaos, Memphis emerged as the beacon of hope for thousands of flood victims from the Bootheel of Missouri to the Mississippi Delta. Coolidge chose Memphis, the largest city in the Mid-South, as the center of rescue and relief operations for the region. The city served as Hoover's headquarters for most of the crisis and the distribution point for reconstruction aid in the months after the flood. The city also became a primary destination for refugees in need of immediate shelter and assistance. Memphians rose to the occasion by offering aid to their fellow Mid-Southerners. Local heroes faced grave dangers in rescuing those stranded by the flood, and some even gave their lives in their efforts.

The flood also left its mark on the environment, politics and society. It changed the political climate of the United States with the election of Hoover as president and forced the federal government to take a greater role in managing the country's rivers with the passage of the subsequent Flood Control Act of 1928. Regionally, the flood caused an increased exodus to northern cities of African Americans disgusted by their second-class status, and in Memphis, the flood provided the opportunity for a political shake-up that would shape local politics for the next twenty-seven years.

The people of Memphis played a central role in rescue, relief and recovery of Mid-Southerners during the Mississippi Valley Flood of 1927. They established a safe haven and relief headquarters without a blueprint to handle a disaster of this magnitude in a time of very limited technology and communications. In fulfilling these roles, Memphians went to extreme measures to help their neighbors, while at the same time protecting their interests and cementing the city's reputation as the Mid-South's most important urban and distribution center. The obstacles they faced and the actions they took help to illuminate their character, their government, their relationship with the rest of the country and their unbreakable connections with the Mid-South.

Chapter 1
THE GREATEST ON RECORD

Who's the one?
Chicago's greatest son
It's Big Bill the Builder!
—1927 campaign song[4]

Mayor William Hale "Big Bill" Thompson of Chicago wanted to celebrate. In January 1927, Congress authorized the construction of a waterway allowing Chicago easier access to New Orleans. Thompson had also recently won a highly contested mayoral race complete with headline-catching scandals and gangland violence. Thompson relished the limelight from his headquarters, but he wanted more. He promised reporters that he would establish an America First Association in every state, he would "show King George V where to get off," he would run the gangsters out of Chicago, he would "make the streets safe so that women and children can go to the movies at night," he would keep the police from "sniffing around for home brew," and he suggested that he might even run for the presidency.[5]

Thompson decided to throw a party, so he chartered two steamboats, the *Cincinnati* and *Cape Girardeau*, to take five hundred guests for a trip down the Mississippi River from Cairo, Illinois, to New Orleans in honor of his reelection and the recent federal legislation. The excursion gave the attention-craving mayor another opportunity to flaunt his victories and feed his appetite for national media attention. Thompson intended to present Mayor Arthur O'Keefe with a raccoon skin nailed to the cabin door of the *Cincinnati* as an emblem of his waterway victory before traveling back to

Chicago with his entourage on April 27 on three special trains consisting of six club cars, six diners and thirty-nine sleeping cars.[6]

On Wednesday, April 20, Thompson and his entourage left Chicago for Cairo on an Illinois Central train named the *Victory Waterway Special*, which consisted of sixteen Pullman cars. Many in the party, including Illinois lieutenant governor Fred E. Sterling and Secretary of State Louis Emmerson, arrived wearing Bill Thompson hats and badges. They found that Big Bill had spared no expense—the two steamers had various forms of entertainment, including eight prizefighters and a fully equipped boxing ring. The *Cape Girardeau* left for Memphis with 125 passengers, followed by the *Cincinnati*, which left with the remainder of the travelers at about 3:00 p.m. Some lesser members of the entourage traveled separately by train in special sleeping cars.[7]

Big Bill and his party steamed down the swollen Mississippi River for a glory cruise, not realizing the disaster that lay ahead. Thompson knew about recent flooding in the Mississippi Valley, but like most people, he did not know the full extent of the calamity. The sympathetic Thompson claimed to have raised $10,000 for flood relief on the train to Cairo. He jokingly told reporters, "Fish sells at twenty-five cents a pound and unless the government does something the farmers will all have to start raising fish!" Thompson's demeanor soon changed. Once underway, the revelers found scenes of complete devastation. A newspaperman from the *Chicago Daily Tribune* traveling with them described scenes of wreckage and ruin and of whole towns submerged, leaving only "roofs and chimneys of houses above the raging river."[8]

Thompson wanted a closer look at the flooding and to offer transportation for flood victims. That night, the *Cape Girardeau* took on sixty refugees at Tomato Islands, Arkansas, including "seven mothers nursing babies at their breasts" and twenty-eight children. Despite the best of intentions, not everyone welcomed the flamboyant Chicago mayor. The U.S. Army Corps of Engineers reported that the waves from the steamers *Cape Girardeau* and the *Cincinnati* "seriously menaced" the levee at Hickman, Kentucky, on April 20. L.Y. Kerr, the engineer in charge, said, "No damage was done, fortunately, but the steamers may be the cause of a big break at some other point if they continue these tactics." Thompson ordered his crews to cut their speed once they found out they could possibly destabilize the strained levees.[9]

Thompson and his associates aboard the steamer "passed the hat" and took up a collection of $1,000 for relief efforts. They arrived in Memphis on April 21 at about 10:00 a.m. and stayed just long enough to deliver the donation. Memphis commissioner Horace Johnson welcomed Thompson's friend Dr. William H. Reid, who carried a letter "conveying the charitable sentiment of the party" and the check for Mayor Rowlett Paine to use "in any way of first aid the mayor might elect."[10]

Unfortunately, the mayors could not meet face-to-face. Thompson had wired Paine the previous day saying that he expected to make it to the city by 5:00 a.m., but river conditions delayed his arrival. Paine normally would have made such a meeting a priority, but what the newspaper called an "emergency" occupied the mayor's attention. He and his newly formed disaster committee scrambled to prepare accommodations for hundreds of refugees fleeing eastern Arkansas and to deal with floodwaters covering the low-lying areas around Memphis.[11]

Problems began in August 1926, when heavy rains drenched Nebraska, South Dakota, Kansas and Oklahoma before moving eastward into Iowa, Missouri, Illinois, Indiana, Kentucky and Ohio. More storms continued for weeks and caused widespread flooding. On September 1, dozens of streams overflowed and flooded towns in a 350-mile area from Carroll, Iowa, to Peoria, Illinois. Three days later, high water deluged much of Nebraska, Kansas, Iowa, Illinois and Indiana, killing four people. The Mississippi River rose rapidly in the upper Midwest, washing out bridges and railroads. Another storm a few days later brought flooding to towns from Terre Haute, Indiana, to Jacksonville, Illinois, killing seven people. The Neosho River rose to record heights and roared through southeastern Kansas, killing five on September 13. The rains continued over almost this entire basin from October through December, with intense snowstorms hitting South Dakota and Montana on December 13.[12]

Heavy rains fell in the lower Mississippi Valley as well. Nearly six inches of rain fell on Little Rock, Arkansas, in one day. In Tennessee, the Cumberland River flooded Nashville and the Tennessee River flooded Chattanooga, killing at least sixteen and leaving thousands homeless over Christmas. On New Year's Day, the Mississippi passed flood stage at Cairo, Illinois, remaining above flood stage for the next 153 days. Rainfall resumed in mid-January, causing river levels to rise again, straining already weakening levees. At Memphis, the Mississippi River began rising on January 1, reaching 37.8 feet on January 12. The water levels lowered to 20.9 feet on January 22 only to begin rising again. The river reached 37.8 feet on February 12, never falling below 30.0 feet through the next month.[13]

The environmental damage from years of deforestation allowed water from these torrential rains to rush directly into streams and eventually the main

Workers reinforce the levee at Lakeport, Arkansas. *Courtesy of Library of Congress.*

channel, causing the river to remain high all winter. Warm weather and early snowmelts caused the upper basin to swell in the beginning of 1927. This was followed by more rain in the upper Midwest, which sent full tributaries gushing into the already swollen Mississippi River. The floodwaters poured down the Mississippi to the Gulf of Mexico with no break in the levee line. The flood crests flowed with such intensity that water backed up into the tributaries, and for a few days the Ohio River actually flowed upstream.[14]

Officials cautiously watched the rivers, while anxious farmers began spring plowing and planting behind the levees. The United States Weather Bureau warned of a spring rise of the Mississippi River, but the Army Corps of Engineers remained confident that their levees would hold back the water. Even so, local levee districts mobilized to monitor and stand ready to repair any breaks.[15]

More bad weather in March worsened the situation in the lower Mississippi Valley. The storms brought Mississippi four inches of rain on March 16, and three tornadoes touched down between March 17 and March 20, killing forty-five people and damaging levees. By the end of the month, every levee board south of Cairo had men patrolling levees twenty-four hours a day on the lookout for breaches. Heavy rains prompted Frederick W. Brist of the National Weather Service at Memphis to issue a warning to Mid-South residents that on March 21 the river would probably reach a flood crest of forty-two feet. He warned owners of livestock and moveable property in low-lying areas to take appropriate actions.[16]

Conditions improved somewhat as water levels in the upper and lower Mississippi River decreased in early April. The Ohio River began to fall, and it appeared as if the tributaries, such as the Wabash, would fall as well. Forecasters updated their predictions and expected the flood stage at Memphis to not exceed forty-one feet. Levees in southern Illinois had weakened, but crews continued to reinforce them. The business section of Hickman, Kentucky, flooded, but the residential section located on the bluffs remained dry. Levees along the St. Francis River in Arkansas, as well as the levees from Tennessee to Louisiana, continued to hold without sand boils or crevasses but remained under constant guard.[17]

Engineers continued to reassure the public that the levees would hold fast. Major J.C.H. Lee, chief of the Third District Corps of Engineers at Vicksburg, said the levees on both sides of the Mississippi River stood firm, and A.E. Markham of the Reelfoot Levee Board reported that levees in Lake County, Tennessee, remained in perfect condition and that Tiptonville was "high and dry." Major Donald H. Connolly, U.S. engineer in charge

Sandbagged boil at Reelfoot levee. *Courtesy of Library of Congress.*

at Memphis, reported that the situation was "exceptionally good" and that all levees held with no immediate indication of a break. He added, "The situation at Columbus, Kentucky does not concern the government. That is a private dyke."[18]

Off the record, however, Connolly, whose district covered 450 miles of river from Cape Girardeau to the mouth of the White River in Arkansas, understood the danger facing the levees and ordered workers to bolster crumbling flood works. He sent additional workers to Laconia Circle, Arkansas, where crews fought rising water and high winds to save the weakening levee. The levee at Burke's Landing, Mississippi, continued to hold after the cave-ins stopped, but the levee break at McClure, Illinois, flooded an area forty miles north of Cairo. Brist maintained his prediction of a forty-two-foot flood stage but would not make a prediction regarding the ultimate flood crest because of the continuing rain.[19]

The ongoing downpours took a heavy toll on the Mid-South, and the *Commercial Appeal* began to describe the outlook as "gloomy." On April 7, watchmen warned residents of Burke's Landing to evacuate when the banks within 75.0 feet of the local levee began to cave in. As rains continued, Brist predicted the flood stage would soon reach 42.5 feet at Memphis. Cairo's flood stage rose three-tenths of a foot overnight to 53.1 feet, and forecasters predicted the flood crest would reach 53.5 feet. On April 9, the roof of S.M.

Naifeh Dry Goods and Department Store in the old Buchanan Building in Hickman, Kentucky, collapsed during a powerful thunderstorm during the night, and Arkansas automobile drivers had to rely on the Choctaw Transportation Service to ferry them between Clarendon and DeVall's Bluff once floodwaters covered the Bankhead Highway.[20]

Levees broke at Lester six miles north of Lake City, Arkansas, and near Kennett, Missouri, on the morning of April 11. Water slowly covered a wide area reaching toward Lundsford and threatened to disrupt train service of the Jonesboro, Lake City and Eastern Railroad. Residents of Marked Tree, Arkansas, held a mass meeting to prepare to fight back the flood. Five thousand sandbags lined the streets before crews transported them to the nearby dam, where two hundred men worked day and night to repair the levee broken in February. A break in Eddyville, Missouri, caused additional water to flow down the Little River, bringing even more floodwater to Marked Tree.[21]

Brist told reporters on April 12, "The future of the high water now depends on the movement of a storm centered today over northwest Texas. If it travels north we will miss further rain. If it goes over the Ohio Valley, there will be another tale to tell." Two days later, the storm system moved toward the Ohio Valley, as the weatherman feared, bringing heavy rain to the Mid-South and surpassing records set in 1913. The flood stage at Cairo reached 55.0 feet, breaking the previous record of 54.7 feet, and meteorologist William E. Barron predicted the gauge would reach 55.5 feet by Sunday. The stage at Memphis rose four-tenths of an inch in twenty-four hours to 42.3 feet, and the rush of floodwater threatened to break the record flood stage at Memphis of 46.6 feet. Transportation officials closed the Little Rock–Memphis highway, and police rerouted traffic to Arkansas City. The main levee protecting Columbus, Kentucky, collapsed at 9:00 a.m. following the second rise of the river. By noon, several feet of water covered the town and interrupted telephone and telegraph services. Major Connolly sent workers with a quarter boat and fifty thousand sacks to reinforce the levee, while families in lower areas behind the levee and in west Hickman began to evacuate.[22]

The situation took a turn for the worse on Good Friday, April 15, when six to fifteen inches of rain fell on an area from Missouri and Illinois, west into Texas, east almost to Alabama and south to the Gulf of Mexico. New Orleans received almost fifteen inches of rain over the course of eighteen hours, totaling over one-quarter of the city's annual average. Newspaper pictures showed downtown New Orleans with four feet of standing water, mistakenly attributing the flooding to Mississippi River overflow rather than heavy rainfall. Greenville, Mississippi, received over eight inches of rain, while neighboring Delta counties received up to fifteen inches. Forecasters at the National Weather Bureau announced that the flood from Cairo to the Gulf of Mexico "will be the greatest on record."[23]

The enormous amount of water caused over two hundred breaks in the mainline levees along the Mississippi River. The overflowing river flooded 170 counties in Illinois, Missouri, Kentucky, Tennessee, Mississippi, Arkansas and Louisiana, covering an area twice the size of Maryland by the time the flood had run its course. When the levees broke, people compared the sound to that of an explosion, thunder or the howling of a wild animal. Some of the worst breaks occurred at New Madrid, Missouri; Mellwood, Arkansas; and Greenville, Mississippi. The lowlands flooded rapidly, leaving twenty-five thousand people seeking refuge in crowded camps.[24]

The flood killed about 250 people immediately, and deaths due to disease and exposure may have numbered over 1,000. Floodwater inundated more than twenty-six thousand square miles, with depths reaching thirty feet and laying waste to cities, towns and farms. It displaced about 700,000 people, destroyed crops and paralyzed industries and transportation, causing an estimated $1 billion in property damage at a time when the federal budget barely exceeded $3 billion. The violent and immense floodwaters drowned people in the fields and in their homes and permanently altered the topography in many areas, including creating a sixty-five-acre lake that remains today as a result of the levee break at Mounds Landing, Mississippi.[25]

Memphis, as the region's primary commercial distribution center, became the logical choice as a headquarters for relief efforts, supplies and news services. The Army Corps of Engineers and Red Cross based their headquarters in Memphis due to the city's proximity to the disaster and its transportation network, which included river, trucking, rail and air facilities. They mobilized military, commercial and private vehicles, while hundreds of volunteers provided manpower and collected donations for refugees. News services arrived and provided the world with up-to-date coverage of the levee breaks, rescue efforts and deaths.

Thousands of desperate flood victims, primarily from Arkansas and Mississippi, rushed to Memphis, making it one of the primary destinations for refugees in the Mid-South. City officials acted quickly to find housing for displaced flood victims in the face of the impending crisis. The mayor suspended all municipal business while his entire staff worked to prepare a camp at the Fairgrounds Amusement Park to house the needy until the floodwaters receded. Memphians had played host to flood victims in the past, but caring for refugees from this flood would prove a greater challenge than any before it.[26]

Chapter 2
WHEN THE LEVEE BREAKS

Cryin' won't help you, praying won't do you no good,
When the levee breaks mama, you've got to move
—Memphis Minnie and Kansas Joe McCoy, "When the Levee Breaks"[27]

The shriek of mill whistles warned of the approaching water. A fifteen-foot wave swept through Clarendon, Arkansas, on April 20, ripping buildings off their foundations and smashing them against trees. Many of the residents scrambled for the high ground of a hilltop cemetery, abandoning their homes and leaving livestock to drown. Others took shelter on the tops of trees and railroad boxcars as the torrent swept by.[28]

A reporter from the Associated Press in New York placed a long-distance call through Memphis to reach the telephone switchboard in the small Arkansas town. Through a shaky connection, telephone operator Rosa Gibson described what happened:

The water is rushing through town. Everything is going before it. As I look out the second-story window, I see everything being washed away. The water was going forty miles per hour this morning. It's slower now, but rising. Cattle, horses, household goods—everything going—it's awful. Boats are rushing to the Negro section. We couldn't warn them yesterday when telephone subscribers were called. They had no phones. Others thought the levee would hold. We don't know what happened to them. Negroes are coming out of the lowlands in boatloads. We don't know how many are drowned. Hundreds are marooned in the courthouse with water rushing around the building. Houseboats from the river were smashed against the building today. Other riverboats—everything on the river—dashed to pieces. Chicken houses, barrels, garages, and small houses are being hurtled along the main street of the town. A boatload of Negroes from the low section of town just came out. They are frightened and screaming. We are trying to keep up with rescue work as far as possible, but we don't know about these poor folks who could not get out. Some of them didn't want to leave their homes—it may be too late for them to leave now, as the water is in the attics of a lot of homes. We hear reports of people screaming everywhere. The water came in during the middle of the night. We warned all we could at 5:00 yesterday, but some of them could not be reached by phone. The levee break came at nearly 2:00 this morning. We expected it. Things here look mighty bad. God knows how much land will be flooded, how many people will be made homeless, and many of them without clothes, and none of them with food. Yes, it's awful, but what can we do?[29]

National Guardsmen from Forrest City arrived at Clarendon on April 21 and found the town in ruins. On May 5, Judge R.F. Milwee of Brinkley; John T. Stimson of the Arkansas Flood Survey and his secretary, Jack Dallmeyer; E.B. Malter of the University of Arkansas; and L.M. Brown of the *Missouri Pacific Lines* magazine arrived in Clarendon on the recently restored railroad. They found that the floodwaters, now receding, had wrecked stores and left perishable goods rotting in the streets. Railroad crews brought lime

Clarendon, Arkansas, after the levee break. *Courtesy of Library of Congress.*

Floodwaters cover homes six miles west of Elaine, Arkansas. *Courtesy of Library of Congress.*

the following day to disinfect and calm the stench. Slime filled the homes, and ruined furniture lined the streets. Crews had to cut part of the levee to release water trapped in the southern part of the town in order to let the remaining water drain.[30]

Rosa Gibson's account reflects what many communities in Arkansas experienced. Almost twice as much farmland flooded in Arkansas as in Mississippi and Louisiana combined in the spring of 1927. Earlier in the year, the White and Little Red Rivers broke through levees in Arkansas, flooding 100,000 acres with ten to fifteen feet of water and leaving five thousand people homeless. Beginning in April, record rainfall fell on Arkansas, with more than seven inches falling on Little Rock in just a few hours. The runoff flowed toward swollen lakes and rivers, unable to drain into the main channel. The swollen Mississippi River backed up into the Arkansas, White and St. Francis Rivers, causing them to run backward and overflow. The streets of Arkansas City in Desha County, dry and dusty at noon, filled with so much water two hours later that "mules were drowning on Main Street faster than people could unhitch them from wagons."[31]

The failure of the levees caused much of Arkansas to remain under water until September. Farmers could not plant crops, and the carcasses of thousands of dead animals lay rotting in stagnant pools. Mosquitoes found perfect conditions to breed, carrying malaria and typhoid to refugee camps already burdened with dysentery and pellagra.[32]

More people than ever before lived in flood zones in Arkansas, as the "buy now, pay later" mindset of the 1920s encouraged farmers to purchase recently cleared riparian land. Heavy machinery enabled the construction of a vast system of levees to hold back rivers, while drainage projects opened up new, low-lying areas left bare by the timber industry. Arkansans borrowed money with easy credit from banks booming with the record levels of the stock market. They expanded their fields to low-lying areas on their own property or moved to new lands fertile from centuries of seasonal flooding.[33]

The success of the farms and the safety of the farmers depended on suitable levees to hold back the rivers from their natural flood zones. The Arkansas General Assembly passed laws between 1905 and 1915 to create a program of flood control in Arkansas' Mississippi River Valley and expand the number of governing drainage districts established in 1881. The drainage districts required landowners to petition the county courts to place a lien on the lands through a court order, ensuring the payment of improvement taxes. Drainage boards used money from taxes to pay the principle and used interest on bonds, along with proceeds from the bond sales, to build levees and drainage canals. The drainage districts also hired deputies to patrol levees and deter sabotage and vandalism. Over time, the crude levees helped transform eastern Arkansas from a "mosquito- and malaria-infested swamp" into rich farmland.[34]

However, the heavy rains and high water of 1927 proved too much for the Arkansas levees. Workers had already labored twenty-five days straight by April 12, when water nearly reached the height of the previous February at the dam near Marked Tree. Industrial plants eventually closed and sent workers to help reinforce the levee. The overflowing Spring River near Hardy washed away a bridge and the Johnson Hickory Mill on April 14. Two hundred workers saved the levee at Tulot as it began to weaken during the afternoon, but during the night a quarter-mile-long section collapsed, allowing floodwaters to sweep in and overtake Trumann. Levees at Bertig failed as well, contributing to the floodwaters that overtook the area extending from the St. Francis River ten miles south of Marked Tree west to Crowley's Ridge.[35]

The Good Friday storms delivered the final blow. Levees at Poplar Bluff and Hornersville, Missouri, broke, sending water into eastern Arkansas. Overflowing water near Conway, Arkansas, threatened to change the course of the Arkansas River and flood much of Faulkner County. One thousand workers tried to close the gap, while Mayor Toney ordered the residents of nearby Pine Bluff to evacuate. On April 17, water broke through levees

Memphis and the Mississippi Valley Flood of 1927

Floodwaters from St. Francis River cover Tulot, Arkansas. *Courtesy of Library of Congress.*

Levee workers on the lower St. Francis River, April 25, 1927. *Courtesy of Library of Congress.*

near Pine Bluff and Plum Bayou near Pastoria and England, flooding over 100,000 acres. Water from the levee breaks around New Madrid, Missouri, flowed south through the Little River into the St. Francis River. H.N. Pharr, chief of the St. Francis Levee Board, warned Marked Tree residents to evacuate and move livestock to higher ground. Another break occurred on April 21 on the Arkansas River at Pendleton, flooding several thousand acres. Water continued to rise as deep as six feet in McGehee, Arkansas City, Tiller, Dumas, Watson, Kelso and McArthur by April 26. Dr. H.H. Rightor of Helena traveled by boat to Arkansas City, where he reported that water ten feet deep covered the town following a levee break at Yoncopin. The town's residents evacuated to a nearby levee and waited for rescue. Flooding caused so much havoc that some communities declared martial law.[36]

Arkansans hardly had time to react. A Gregory bus barely made it across the Little Crow Creek Bridge on Bankhead Highway between Forrest City and Madison before it washed away. The two hundred residents of McClelland fled to Cotton Plant as floodwaters fifteen to twenty feet deep struck their town and washed away seventy of the seventy-five homes. The remains of the town splintered downriver against a railroad trestle. A woman with six small children barely made it to safety before collapsing after paddling her skiff to shore. However, another resident, Jim Goff, did not leave in time and drowned when his skiff overturned in the powerful floodwaters.[37]

Those who ignored the warnings to evacuate often paid dearly. Twelve miles east of Little Rock, neighbors on higher ground warned three families living on the nearby Flynn Plantation about the coming flood. "Think we'll stay—river won't get near us," they answered. Late that night, neighbors saw lights and heard screams from the plantation. Soon the lights went out and the voices silenced. In the morning, deep water covered where three houses once stood. C.C. Simon's four-year-old daughter fell from her porch and drowned in Mellwood, Arkansas, on April 5. Two Little Rock children, Lonnie White (thirteen) and Floella McDonald (eleven), drowned trying to cross a creek on the way home from school on April 17. On the same day, John Dixon, an African American farmer, drowned near Madisonville. His two sons escaped by keeping afloat on a raft of logs until rescuers saved them. Another resident, Lonnie Mathis, drowned when his skiff overturned while trying to locate his parents. The Little Rock newspaper reported fifteen more deaths on April 20: three-year-old Julius Lamb fell from his porch in Trumann into floodwater; twenty-four-year-old E. Rainwater drowned at Morrillton; three unnamed African American men drowned and nine others went missing when their six skiffs towed by a motorboat capsized near a levee break; and another African American man drowned near Bradley.[38]

Floodwaters disrupted communications, leaving many communities isolated. Three to four feet of floodwater blocked the Frisco Railroad's main Memphis–Kansas City line at Black Rock, Arkansas. The flooding knocked out most telephone and telegraph service through the state by April 20. Floodwaters even began to damage the road into Memphis. Arkansas highway commissioner Dwight H. Blackwood and Judge Renfro Turner of Crittenden County, realizing the gravity of the flood control problem, met at the Peabody Hotel in Memphis to discuss joint control of the Harahan Viaduct and replacing the earthen structure with concrete to better withstand flooding.[39]

By April 19, eleven thousand of the twenty-five thousand refugees in the Mississippi Valley had taken shelter in makeshift Arkansas Red Cross camps that suffered from lack of shelter, supply shortages and isolation. Those fortunate enough to make it to the camps lived for months in tents with little to protect them from the extreme changes in the weather. On April 21, temperatures at Bentonville dropped from seventy-six degrees to forty degrees overnight. Thousands of homeless, hungry and ill from exposure, remained stranded in Pine Bluff after floodwaters interrupted transportation in and out of the city. Cotton Plant, the primary destination for many refugees escaping flood-ravaged McClellan, soon became cut off from the outside as well. Mayor Trice called state militia for rescue work, while residents built barracks to shelter refugees.[40]

Marianna, still safe due to its location on Crowley's Ridge, had provided shelter for over 1,500 refugees by April 20. The numbers grew steadily as more arrived by Missouri Pacific trains and river steamers. Those arriving by gas boats reported seeing hundreds of people and livestock stranded on isolated mounds of land. The government towboat *Augustine* and steamer *Harry Lee* made repeated trips into the flooded areas to pick up the stranded, and by April 22 the town housed over 3,000 refugees. Residents of nearby Brickeys evacuated after floodwaters reached the town following the levee break ten days earlier at Whitehall, where at least five people drowned. Farmers saved most of their livestock but lost all their planting seed. Flooding cut off all communications except for a single telephone in the second story of the Missouri Pacific Railroad Station, where agent H.E. Friend could send only outgoing calls.[41]

Forrest City, also on Crowley's Ridge, had over five thousand flood victims in the city by April 20. The number soon doubled, making Forrest City the largest refugee camp in Arkansas. Cut off from the outside world, the local

Backwater from L'Anguille River floods Brickeys, Arkansas. *Courtesy of Library of Congress.*

Red Cross struggled to find tents and food for the steady stream of flood victims who soon outnumbered the local population two to one. Helen Colwell, experienced in directing disaster relief in Florida, arrived from Chicago to oversee operations. She oversaw the care of 10,929 refugees with the help of the Memphis Red Cross, which supplied six gas-powered, flat-bottomed boats and crewmen, including P.A. Mitchell, H.W. Bailey, M.C. Barnesworth, E.L. Preston, Carl Smith, Eugene Warren and A.L. Stevens. Colwell and the volunteers traveled hundreds of miles through St. Francis and Crittenden Counties delivering supplies and rescuing the stranded.[42]

Over 82,000 refugees remained in camps in Arkansas at the beginning of May: Fort Smith, 700; Paris, 350; Russellville, 500; Dardanelle, 350; Little Rock, 1,500; England, 3,000; Stuttgart, 1,390; Pine Bluff, 400; Blytheville, 4,500; Jonesboro, 550; New Port, 300; Marked Tree, 800; Forrest City, 12,870; Brinkley, 4,500; Marianna, 3,500; Hughes, Seyppel and Bruin, 6,200; Helena, 12,000; Selma, 740; Monticello, 6,000; Wilmar, 4,000; Warren, 5,000; McGehee, 1,200; Line, 350; Hamburg, 600; Jerome, 300; and Eudora, 2,750. These refugees could only look forward to returning to miles of watery desolation covering their homes and possessions. Red Cross disaster relief director Henry Baker, who oversaw the steady flow of supplies

Red Cross director Henry M. Baker. *Courtesy of Library of Congress.*

into Arkansas, said, "No man can exaggerate the seriousness of what has and is taking place—[it] staggers imagination."[43]

Water pressure and high winds threatened levees from the Kentucky/Tennessee state line down to Shelby County. Assistant U.S. Engineer C.E.

Huffstetter, who supervised flood control at Reelfoot Lake in 1922, returned to direct levee operations. He found that the continuous rain and an inadequate spillway caused water to back up and flood thousands of acres of Tipton County, reaching within one foot of the top of the levee. Rumors circulated that Kentuckians planned to dynamite levees, so Huffstetter requested help from the Tennessee National Guard. By April 21, thirty guardsmen patrolled the levee to deter any possible saboteurs. Despite the engineers' work, floodwater eventually found its way through weak spots and covered two-thirds of Lauderdale County, leaving over one thousand homeless.[44]

The single worst levee break occurred at Scott's Landing near the site of Huntingdon, Mississippi, an old ferry town that had washed away in a flood thirty years earlier. Thousands of African American men worked frantically to reinforce the weakening levee—also known as Stop's Landing, Mound's Landing or Moore's Landing—but despite all their efforts, a three-hundred-foot section of the levee collapsed about 7:30 a.m. on April 21. Warning blasts from the Mississippi Power and Light plant's whistle warned residents of the break. The crevasse had grown to over half a mile wide by the evening, sweeping away many of the workers and flooding over three

Flood refugees in Leland, Mississippi. *Courtesy of the University of Mississippi Archives and Special Collections.*

thousand miles. The citizens of Scott used every available automobile to transport white women and children to safety. The Yazoo and Mississippi Valley (Y&MV) Railroad supplied two boxcars to move all the African American women and children to Cleveland, Mississippi.[45]

The water from the Scott's Landing break swept through the town of Paducah, Mississippi, smashing homes and buildings and stranding survivors in trees and on rooftops. The bellowing of Ernest Clark's doomed cattle warned him of the approaching water. Clark managed to get his wife, mother-in-law and four children in a boat as the water hit his home. The wave struck the small boat, smashing it to pieces, and carried away his family. The water washed Clark into a barbed wire fence, where he became entangled. Sinking under the waves, Clark managed to break free. Badly cut, he floated downstream to a treetop where his family struggled against the current. The family tried to hold on, but the exhausted women and children eventually lost their grips and fell into the water before Clark could pull them back. Clark said, "I attempted to save them, but they were caught in a current that seemed to be traveling at twenty-five miles an hour. Before I could extend a hand to them they were swept away. I saw them sink twice, then the third time, my wife, God bless her, called out to save myself. It is so terrible I believe it will kill me." Clark's wife, Valeria, survived, but the others were not so fortunate. Clark believed only he had survived until William Miller and Turner Dunn, two rescue workers from Clarksdale, found him three days later and reunited him with his wife in Greenville.[46]

Photographer Frank "Pinky" Hitchings, correspondent John C. Ottinger Jr. and L.K. Salsbury traveled through flood-ravaged Mississippi to get pictures and stories for the *Memphis Evening Appeal*. They arrived at Scott's Landing to see the massive levee break and the damage it caused. They found survivors and cattle gathered on the remains of the levee in the "lowest state of dejection." People from all walks of life gathered on the levees—the highest ground in the vicinity. Ottinger recalled seeing "White and Negro, plantation masters and vassal Negroes" without food and water. Floodwaters

Refugees and livestock share a piece of dry land. *Courtesy of the University of Mississippi Archives and Special Collections.*

ruined food supplies and filled the artesian wells, fouling the drink water supply. Children cried for water, and only the most desperate risked contracting typhoid fever by drinking river water. Refugees started fires for warmth at five or six points along the concrete-topped levee, but the fires had little effect and the smoke only added to their discomfort. Now and again someone would start a song, but no one would join the chorus so the pitiful spark of enthusiasm soon sputtered out.[47]

Governor Dennis Murphree made a personal plea for federal aid to President Coolidge, Secretary of War Davis and Major General Malin Craig of the Fourth Corps. Murphree said, "The situation in Mississippi has grown beyond the control of the local and state authorities. Every possible assistance of the state of Mississippi is being given, but the task is simply too great." Coolidge handed responsibility over to the Red Cross, which soon located its headquarters in Memphis. The agency quickly collected materials such as food, medicine and boats for transportation.[48]

Relief workers traveling along levee tops arrived in Ford trucks to distribute scanty rations. Women and children received the first of the sandwiches of stale bread and musty cheese. A barge finally arrived at 11:00 p.m.—six hours late. National guardsmen ordered "women and children first" before allowing any men aboard for the journey to Vicksburg. They traveled almost in silence, except for the commotion caused by the birth of child on the barge carrying African Americans. Hitchings noted, "There was scarce a noise save the swish of the waters. It might have been a cargo of souls crossing the Styx in darkness in penetrating cold."[49]

A steady stream of supplies and equipment soon began arriving from the Memphis Red Cross headquarters. Cleveland, Mississippi relief agencies caring for refugees from the Scott's Landing levee break received blankets and quilts for the three thousand refugees after they sent an urgent request to the *Memphis Evening Appeal*. Twenty motorboats and seventy-five skiffs arrived by rail at Scott's Landing from Memphis on April 22. Crews used the watercrafts to transport the remaining African American workers stranded on roofs, sawmills, cotton gins and office buildings to the refugee camp at Beeson. L.K. Salsbury, president of Delta and Pine Land Company, said, "Our property loss has been tremendous. The water was fifteen feet at Scott near the broken levee. Hundreds of head of livestock have been swept away in the flood and buildings destroyed. My great worry, however, has been for our Negro employees, and I am thankful to know we will be able to take care of them without any deaths."[50]

Water from the Scott's Landing levee break caused the worst flood in Greenville since 1903. Mayor of Greenville John Aloysius Cannon wrote, "We were somewhat late in turning on the alarm, as we could get no one at the Levee Board with the proper authority to say where the break was." The whistle finally warned the residents of Greenville about the broken levee. Before long, Greenville resembled Venice, as a sea of water soon covered the commercial and residential areas. Citizens either rowed down the streets and avenues or walked on the raised walkways. Many of the town's citizens had prepared their homes and businesses for the high water by pulling up carpets and placing furniture and goods on raised platforms. Others immediately began fleeing

Greenville, Mississippi, April 30, 1927. *Courtesy of the University of Mississippi Archives and Special Collections.*

Floodwaters from the Scott's Landing levee break cover Greenville. *Courtesy of the University of Mississippi Archives and Special Collections.*

the area by train until floodwaters made the tracks unusable. Steamboats then carried many of the white wives and young children away to Vicksburg or Memphis, leaving behind African Americans to work the levees and unload steamers.[51]

Mayor Paine's disaster committee and the Red Cross provided much-needed equipment. City alderman Joe Weinberg traveled to Memphis on April 26 to request the use of a fire pumper after eight feet of water disabled the Greenville waterworks, making the local fire engine unusable. Paine generously sent by boat a crew and a gasoline-operated pumper that could use river water. A few days later, Colonel Spalding of the Army Corps of Engineers ordered another fleet of motorboats to Greenville to assist in rescuing people near the Sunflower

River and Yazoo Valley. A steady flow of supplies and relief workers soon followed. Greenville's citizens quickly cleaned up parts of their downtown as the flood crest passed, and Red Cross representative Wally West of Washington County traveled to Memphis to make plans to reestablish regular commercial and passenger transportation.[52]

Communities in the Yazoo Basin had an especially difficult time maintaining order because of looting in towns and surrounding farms. National guardsmen enforced martial law and curfews in Greenville, and Belzoni law enforcement held five looters in the county jail without bond. On May 2, the Yazoo City council met with the local chamber of commerce and agreed to request additional national guardsmen to help police control over seven hundred African American men wandering the streets. Authorities encouraged them to go to the Red Cross camps, but the men refused, preferring to sleep in alleys and around public buildings. Suspicious residents became even more anxious when they lost power and the city became almost completely dark after nightfall. Five-foot-deep water forced the evacuation of the more affluent neighborhoods, whose residents feared the homeless refugees would break into abandoned homes.[53]

Unscrupulous plantation owners used the chaotic situation to their advantage by having labor agents lure displaced field workers away from their neighbors' farms. Yazoo residents claimed that labor agents circulated stories among African Americans of mistreatment in refugee camps in order to mislead them into agreeing to work on competing plantations in adjacent counties. Agents took those who agreed to follow them into the hills, where farmers recruited them as labor in exchange for money. On one occasion in early May, an African American man asked Yazoo Red Cross workers to let him back into the refugee camp after he claimed that a white man gave him a forged release form stating he owned land, which exempted him from having to report to the camp. The field hand realized the agent only wanted to place him on a different plantation and decided to return.[54]

The Mississippi flood dictator L.O. Crosby appointed Memphis-born Jeptha Fowlkes Barbour, attorney and vice-president of the Delta National Bank, to convince African American refugees to "turn a deaf ear to the propaganda of the labor agents." Barbour, along with several black preachers, spoke at Camp Quekemeyer and tried to convince refugees to remain in the camps and eventually return to their assigned plantations. Governor Murphree and General Green also called on all Mississippi camps to "refrain from allowing the moving of labor." Even so, some residents preferred direct action. A representative of the Yazoo Vigilance

Refugees at a Red Cross camp in Cleveland, Mississippi. *Courtesy of the University of Mississippi Archives and Special Collections.*

Committee warned that "labor agents will be dealt with on the old time Yazoo plan." On at least one occasion, alleged labor agents barely escaped across the county after armed vigilantes pursued them in a high-speed car chase.[55]

Delta communities such as Leland remained under water for months, even with the passage of the flood crest. On May 21, *Commercial Appeal* reporter George Moreland traveled from Greenville with attorney B.B. Carmichael to see firsthand the condition of Leland. They found much of the town damaged and still covered by four to seven feet of water. Holes in roofs indicated where people cut their way through to escape the sudden rush of water, ugly drifts lodged against buildings and a stench rose from flooded houses. Residents finally pumped water out of the town once they repaired the broken levee. Homeowners returned as soon as water fell below their floors only to find their furniture and other possessions covered in stinking, yellow mud. Moreland wrote, "It requires the courage of Hannibal to face the conditions which exist in this city. It requires brave hearts to tackle the task of rehabilitation when such havoc has been wrought."[56]

However, those with the least suffered the most. Eighteen-year-old Richard Wright lived in Memphis at the time of the flood and saw the rising waters and the steady stream of refugees escaping Arkansas. A decade later, the author wrote *The Man Who Saw the Flood* (1937) and *Down by the Riverside* (1938), which he based on interviews with former refugees at the Chicago John Reed Club. They illustrate the hardships experienced by African American sharecroppers because of the flood and contradict a "truism so prevalent in popular literature and the press describing the flood experience of 1927: that the commonality of the experience led to unity, cooperation, and goodwill between the races."[57]

Author Pete Daniel wrote that the flood "revealed that seventy-five years after emancipation white Southerners continued to hold Black laborers in bondage." Planters did this by manipulating one-sided work arrangements with poor tenant farmers. During the antebellum era, planters used slaves as collateral when securing credit from merchants to purchase essential supplies. At the end of the Civil War, planters lost up to $3 billion in private property because of the uncompensated emancipation of the slaves. According to historian Robyn Spencer, "the desperate search for credit in this cash-poor system shaped post-Emancipation economic relationships in such a way that both planter and Black agricultural laborer were bound together in a complex web of dependency, negotiation, and struggle. One crucial strand of this web was sharecropping."[58]

Sharecroppers, owning no tools or livestock, labored for planters in return for a share of the proceeds from the sale of the harvested crop. The sharecropping system allowed planters to advance credit at inflated prices to tenants through the plantation store, the only accessible source for necessary supplies. Following the harvest, the plantation store clerks deducted the amount owed from the sharecroppers' share. The arrangement perpetually bound the workers to the planters since their earnings rarely covered their debt. Their accounts grew progressively worse every season, giving the planters an excuse to force the workers to stay. If sharecroppers tried to run away, they risked imprisonment, beating or death at the hands of local law enforcement. Essentially, the system kept the sharecroppers in a state of slavery.[59]

The flood proved especially difficult for African American sharecroppers. Rescue workers often ignored them, leaving them stranded on the few remaining pieces of dry land. Law enforcement forced many at gunpoint to stay on levees, where they waited in vain in makeshift tents for transportation. Rescuers picked up whites—and even mules—before blacks in some cases.[60]

It took four months for the floodwaters to recede, and during that time sheriff's deputies and national guardsmen kept thousands of landless African American sharecroppers confined in Red Cross refugee camps in Mississippi and Arkansas to ensure they would eventually return to the plantations where they worked. Planters feared that their sharecroppers, deep in debt, would not return from the Red Cross camps, leaving them without enough labor to put crops in the fields once the land dried out. Armed guards directed the workers into labor details in exchange for meager food and supplies and beat those who would not work. Local police rounded up those who refused to go to the camps and forced them to work unloading supplies on the levees.[61]

In mid-September, the Red Cross allowed the sharecroppers to return to their devastated land to try to survive the winter and start over with virtually nothing. Thousands, tired of farming, poverty and debt, left the plantations as soon as they could, heading north to look for jobs in cities such as Detroit and Chicago. Historian Robyn Spencer discovered an account of one exhausted Arkansas refugee in Memphis, whose callous mistreatment exemplified many African Americans' experience during the flood. The man appealed for help to the owner of the plantation where he had worked most of his life:

> *Year after year I have raised the best crops I could and spent as little for supplies as I could. I have never complained though I knowed he wasn't treating me right. But when the flood came and I had to wade in water up to my neck holding my grandchildren high over my head to save them, I appealed to this white man to help me save my family and he said to me "Don't bring your troubles to me." I will never go back to Arkansas again.*[62]

Secretary Hoover and James L. Fieser, vice-chairman of the American National Red Cross, announced the policy of a "square deal for all." They appointed a seventeen-member commission headed by Dr. Robert R. Moton, principal of the Tuskegee Institute, to investigate complaints from African American refugees and to make suggestions for improvement in methods and administration. The Colored Advisory Commission, meeting at Memphis on June 2, launched investigations into the conditions in the refugee camps and later reported to Hoover and Fieser at Baton Rouge, Louisiana. Hoover stated in his telegram to Moton on May 24:

> *With a view to making certain the proper treatment of the colored people in the concentration camps of the flood district and with a view to inquire into any complaints, I would like you to advise me as to the appointment of a commission of representative colored citizens who can visit these camps and who can make investigation of any complaint or criticisms. Fieser who is the acting head of the Red Cross joins me in this request.*[63]

Walter White of the NAACP requested that Hoover break up the camps, which he referred to as slave labor penitentiaries where officials tagged sharecroppers with their names and the names of the plantation owners for whom they worked. On April 30, Sidney Dillon Redmond, a prominent black physician, lawyer, businessman and member of the Colored Advisory Commission, complained about peonage being practiced on a massive scale. He described how national guardsmen kept African Americans prisoner in camps until they were forced to return to plantations.[64]

Hoover exploded when Moton informed him of the forced conscription of African Americans at gunpoint to work on the levees and the beatings and murders by soldiers. The secretary refused to believe the stories and insisted that Moton rewrite his report. He did not want anything to ruin the picture of the virtues of volunteerism, private charity and local control.[65]

Hoover also had hopes of becoming president and feared the negative press from the refugee camps might hurt his candidacy. On August 8, *Time* magazine ran the following story, obviously written to contradict reports from the refugee camps and to generate political support for Hoover's White House aims:

> *In Arkansas, Negroes flooded from the plantations arranged a Hoover celebration, presented him with a loving cup. On the cup was inscribed: Presented to Hon. Herbert Hoover in token of appreciation and gratitude for his wonderful work and sympathy during flood of 1927 by the Colored People of Arkansas. One of the Negroes was quoted as having said: "Sho' would have had a hard time didn't Mr. Hoover come to fetch us to de high ground...sho' would make a noble president." And a white man was said to have remarked: "We think Hoover is the most useful American of his day. Why, he'd make a fine president."*[66]

African Americans played an important role in the Republican National Convention even though they could not vote in most elections in the South. According to the historian John Barry, Hoover, to protect himself from charges of neglect and to secure core delegates, reached a deal with the national African American leadership by appointing the Colored Advisory Commission to investigate the abuses. Hoover promised to break large plantations into small farms and turn sharecroppers into owners if the commission whitewashed the scandals and supported his candidacy. Commission members kept their word, but Hoover broke his, injuring the party's relationship with African Americans and helping to eventually push them to the Democratic Party.[67]

Along the river, numerous refugee camps sprang up where refugees huddled in public buildings or tents, living as captives waiting for the waters to subside. Even in Memphis, city officials created a refugee sanctuary that also functioned in effect as a prison camp. The *Commercial Appeal* reported that the "camp is closed to the public…no one is permitted to enter or leave the grounds except on passes from headquarters."[68]

Chapter 3
HIGHER GROUND

All day, all night, the ceaseless beat of hoofs,
Of mules, of cattle, through the city's mart,
As homeless now as we, led out to seek
the shelter that the willing stranger lends.
Where now we stand was once our market place,
We bought and sold our wares as other men;
But now, 'tis but the refuge place of those
who, losing all they had, would still keep hope.
—*Virginia Frazer Boyle, "The Breaking of the Levee"*

The whistle blew for the afternoon's program at the Tri-State Fairgrounds. However, instead of the usual crowds of locals in attendance, the audience consisted entirely of flood refugees. The mayor of Memphis ordered the facility closed to the general public so that the Red Cross could use it as a refugee camp. Now it served as a temporary home to over two thousand people waiting to return to their flood-ravaged homes.

Susie Larry, who oversaw entertainment, recreation and camp school, watched as the crowd gathered. African American refugees, many with improvised fans, took their seats on bleachers under a clear and sunny sky to sing along with the spirituals led by members of the African Methodist Church. Mothers rocked small children and babies to the rhythm of the chants, while the more restless children, with their flapping shoes and cut-off trousers or faded dresses, quietly played.[69]

A routine set in for the refugees shortly after their arrival in the camp. Following "bath day," they received clean clothes after their turns in the showers at the swimming pool between the midday and last meal at four o'clock. The transportation department steadily delivered newly arrived refugees, baggage and livestock to the camp throughout the day and night. The Red Cross also kept an ambulance on hand to deliver expectant mothers and others in need of medical attention to the hospital. Relief workers cared for the animals as well. They quartered livestock in the fairgrounds swine barn, and Mrs. D.G. Allen offered to keep any dogs free of charge at her residence a few blocks away on Greer Street until the flood passed.[70]

African American workers began preparing food for the first meal at 8:00 a.m. However, many of the camp's residents formed lines outside the "grub houses" long before messengers went to the sleeping quarters to announce meals. Refugees presented identification badges with their names and hometowns in order to receive cups of buttermilk and tin plates of eggs, corn bread, sweet potatoes, meat stew, black-eyed peas and white bread. Workers distributed apples, candy, cookies and cake in the living quarters afterward, and refugees could get chewing and smoking tobacco after meals. The refugees appreciated the food, shelter and kindness offered, but they still felt a sense of anxiety. They wondered what would happen when the waters receded. What could be done when so many had lost everything?[71]

Returning from his tour of the flooded Mississippi Valley, James L. Fieser, vice-chairman of the American National Red Cross, wrote: "I have just seen at firsthand one of the most staggering tragedies this country has ever suffered." He believed that the flood exceeded the devastation of the 1900 Galveston flood, the 1906 San Francisco earthquake, the South Carolina tornado of 1923, the northern Ohio tornado of 1924, the midwestern tornado of 1925 and the Florida hurricane of the previous September. The Red Cross cared for about thirty thousand people following the tornado of 1925, spending approximately $3 million, and it had spent just over $4 million to care for eighty thousand people following the hurricane in 1924. According to Fieser, the Red Cross currently cared for twice that many, with the number growing daily.[72]

Fieser recounted seeing thousands of men working nonstop in the mud to bolster weakening levees. As the levees failed, these workers gathered their families and what possessions they could carry and fled to higher ground. Others chose to stay in their homes, suffering in the confines of upper stories while waiting for Red Cross provisions. Children suffered the most. Fieser wrote, "Perhaps the most tragic part of the whole story is the plight of the thousands of children, hapless little pawns in the hands of the flood, who have been crowded into refugee camps. Bewildered, dazed, and unable to comprehend the situation, they come clinging desperately to dolls, toys, and other trivial articles which in happier days brought them such delight."[73]

Phil Green, along with his wife, two-year-old son and cousin Bonnie Lee Culver, arrived in Memphis with the first of the refugees from Arkansas. Mrs. Culver said, "Some time ago the man who owns the land we farm came and told us to look out for floods. Day before yesterday he came again and told us to look out, that we better move on, as the place would be under water. Nearly everybody has left Heth." The family calmly loaded their mule team with their household goods and prepared a picnic basket. They arrived at the Salvation Army headquarters in Memphis that evening. Green planned to give up Arkansas and stay in Memphis to get a job. They also reported passing "dozens of Negroes" carrying their belongings headed for Memphis. These included Arkansans from Whitehall and Proctor, as well as thirteen sharecroppers from the plantation of Memphis broker F.C. Weatherby in Fifteen Mile Bayou.[74]

Unlike the Greens, who left early, most of the refugees did not leave their homes until floodwaters swept through their communities. For days, the caravan of the destitute wound its way out of the mire, mud and water of Arkansas. The biting wind off the river added to the misery of scores of half-clad refugees. Families huddled together in tents along the way, bereft of all their worldly possessions but thankful to escape with their lives. They arrived by train, boat, wagon or automobile or straggled in on foot near exhaustion from the long battle with the flood and lack of sleep and food.[75]

Some Memphians offered to take in refugees. On April 20, Phil and Joe Conley, owners of Dinty Moore's Grocery, offered shelter and food for refugees at their store free of charge. Captain Widgery took in eighty-six refugees at the Salvation Army men's quarters on Third Street, and Dick Turner, proprietor of Gehring's Hotel at Eighty-four Union Avenue, offered to let refugees use fifteen of his rooms. Captain Will Lee of the Memphis Police Department appreciated Turner's offer but said, "We are trying to house them all at the Fairgrounds so that we can keep them together. It is much easier to feed them there and in case of sickness we can keep them from spreading disease."[76]

On April 19, the local chapters of the Red Cross and American Legion met with Mayor Paine, the park commission and officials from the Tri-State Fair Commission to prepare for the thousands of refugees expected to arrive in Memphis. They closed the Tri-State Fairgrounds amusement park to the public and converted it into a refugee camp—just as the city had done during the catastrophic flood of 1913. The mayor's new disaster committee then assigned duties to various members of the agencies. Commissioners John Waddell, Jack Carley and Major Jesse Gaston used a boat provided by Major Connolly of the Army Corps of Engineers to rescue flood victims. Waddell also oversaw the transportation of refugees to the camp with the help of Robert Hugo and Bert Bates. City health officer Dr. J.J. Durrett acted as the camp sanitary officer, and W.B. Bayless, head of the local Red Cross, and Colonel Roane Waring, commander of the local American Legion, ran the overall operation. Other officials included: Walker Taylor, executive officer, assisted by A.L. Tate and Jack Carley; Captain H.B. Smith, quartermaster; W.B. Spurling, requisition and liaison; Paul Jones and Marshall Yandel, registration; W.H. Bedford and W.P. Rhea, personal and discipline assistants; A.B. Carpenter and Claude Schultz, bedding and housing assistants; John E. McCall and Melville Joy, property assistants; and Charles Cox and Harry Light, commissary assistants in charge of purchases, supplies and cooking.[77]

The city's mayor, Rowlett Paine, faced the greatest challenge of his career. He wanted to live up to the expectations of his constituency and protect his hometown. In 1919, the executive committee of the Citizen's League drafted Paine as a candidate to appeal to the city's business elite. Upon his election, Paine, the "businessman's mayor," presided over the building of Ellis Auditorium and a series of viaducts that would speed traffic by passing over railroad tracks. He also worked to bring the University of Tennessee Medical School to Memphis. Paine managed pay raises for teachers, successfully led the city through a fire strike, resisted a recall movement and promoted city planning. He had every intention of preserving the image of the city and avoiding the kind of chaos happening in Greenville and other communities.[78]

The Red Cross Midwest headquarters in St. Louis requested that officials detain refugees headed for Memphis in hopes that camps in Arkansas would care for refugees. However, conditions in the makeshift camps soon deteriorated. The mayor and his disaster committee knew that the flood would soon drive hundreds of refugees to Memphis, so they put a plan into place that would allow them to maintain control of the inevitable arrival of these desperate and possibly dangerous people. At 4:00 p.m. on April 21, Paine received a call from William C. Rapp, superintendent of the Union Railway Company, notifying him that two trainloads of refugees would soon arrive over the Missouri Pacific Railroad. Paine immediately dispatched his secretary, Jack Carley, and a police detail to meet the train at Briark, Arkansas, and conduct it into the city. Major M. Crawford of the

Mayor Rowlett Paine. *Courtesy of the Memphis and Shelby County Room, Memphis Public Library and Information Center.*

U.S. Army volunteered to lead another police detail to meet a second train. Paine ordered both trains to unload their passengers at Central Avenue and Parkway about a block from the fairgrounds. City shops foreman Walter Trent directed crews to load the refugees' belongings into six trucks for transfer to the camp, where Chief of Police Burney ordered policemen to

Floodwater from the St. Francis River covers Hughes, Arkansas. *Courtesy of Library of Congress.*

guard the facility around the clock. The camp soon began to fill to capacity as another thousand refugees arrived in Memphis by train from Hughes and Hulbert on April 23.[79]

Carley and Detective Sergeant William Raney set up a tent as a checkpoint at the Harahan Bridge to intercept refugees on foot or in vehicles as they entered Memphis. Eight motorcycle police officers escorted refugees to the fairgrounds to keep them from wandering around the city. The police also kept two trucks on hand to either drive refugees to the camp or go to Arkansas to pick up those stranded by the flood. On the evening of April 24, eight families arrived from a flooded area between Hughes and Briark. Major Crawford and eight soldiers provided first aid, food and clothing for refugees until they could move to the fairgrounds refugee camp. They set up a telephone connection with Hulbert in order to receive calls to evacuate flood victims within twelve miles of the camp.[80]

By April 24, the fairgrounds camp held 1,060 refugees, with more on the way. The previous night, 500 had appeared in the city, and 1,000 appeared the following day, arriving "half-clad, caked with mud and in a dazed condition from the sudden loss of all their worldly possessions." The Red Cross provided tents, clothing, food and other supplies, while Waring's men cooked meals, provided transportation, passed out supplies and maintained discipline. The National Guard 115th Field Artillery brought rolling food kitchens and set them up in the fairgrounds' church booths. The U.S. Army Fourth Corps in Atlanta sent blankets, cots and 1,200 one-man tents. Camp officials planned to put two refugees in each tent so that they could accommodate up to 2,400.[81]

Waring operated the camp along military lines, especially in regards to sanitation, discipline and work details. He ordered gates locked and closed the park to the public. Camp officials, made up of Red Cross and American Legion members, met refugees at boat docks and the train station and transported them directly to the fairgrounds, where they remained under guard. Refugees used the showers at the swimming pool and received new overalls while volunteers washed their clothes. Once the refugees received clean clothes, camp officials issued identification tags and medical staff gave vaccinations. The Red Cross then segregated the refugees by race, placing white families in the automobile building and African American families in the stock building. Camp officials then sent male refugees in good condition to work on the levees for $1.50 a day, while women stayed behind to help maintain the camp by sweeping and mopping floors with antiseptics.[82]

Waring issued revised rules for the fairgrounds camp on April 25. The refugees had to present registration cards to receive meals, which were given at 8:00 a.m. and 4:00 p.m., and to gain access to their assigned sleeping quarters. Officials moved the white refugees to the merchants' building, where families made sleeping quarters in the miniature stores used by merchants during the fair. Additional African American refugees moved into the automobile and Shelby County buildings. Police only allowed visitors with passes issued from the Red Cross headquarters access to the camp.[83]

Eventually, the camp became so crowded that the Red Cross took over the recently opened Ellis Auditorium to process refugees and sort donations. City officials had hoped to inaugurate the facility to Memphians on a more celebratory note. Squire J.J. McNamara asked fellow members of the Shelby County Court on April 18 to attend a gathering at the auditorium sponsored by the North Memphis Civic Improvement Club. Planners organized a series of dances as a way to introduce Memphians to the new facility. However, the flood crisis took precedence, and relief workers took the place of dancers in the facility's first official function. The American Legion filmed the relief staff at the auditorium on May 6, capturing them in every aspect of their work. Howard P. Savage, American Legion national commander, sent a letter to Memphis Post No. 1 congratulating the members on their efforts. He referred to their spirit of service and self-sacrifice as "well worthy of warriors."[84]

Officials of the camp in Memphis, unlike its counterparts elsewhere in the region, took steps to treat African American refugees with some degree of consideration. Waring appointed DeWitt T. Alcorn to supervise relief to African American refugees. Alcorn called together a committee including Dr. T.O. Fuller, Dr. L.G. Patterson, Reverend A.L. DeMond, Reverend J.L. Campbell, Reverend S.A. Owens, Dr. D.J. Thomas and Dr. S.W. Brown who met at the gate of the fairgrounds at noon on April 22 to evaluate the needs of the refugees. Regardless of whether Alcorn's efforts were voluntary or the result of pressure from the African American community, the refugees received somewhat better treatment in Memphis than in most camps in the Mid-South.[85]

The morale of the refugees at the fairgrounds camp sank despite the best efforts of Susie Larry's entertainment committee. Playgrounds superintendent Robert O'Brien appealed to the Council of Social Agencies to help recruit more entertainers to help the flood victims "forget their troubles." Children learned folk dances and played games furnished by the city's Parks and Recreation Department. J.L. Highsaw, principal of Crockett Technical School, provided a movie projector, and a local store donated a radio. The Tech High School Band and Glee Club, Knights of Columbus Band, Elk's Club Band, Pullman Porter's Band and Royal Circle Band all provided musical shows. The camp also had religious services and schools for the children. Crews set up additional mess halls and moved the kitchen to larger facilities. The Scottish Rite's DeMolay Boys, under the direction of Phil Hacker, performed for the refugees at the fairgrounds and Oakville Sanitarium on April 24. On May 2, Edward M. Salomon, vice-president of Bry's Department Store, dressed in a suit and straw hat, arrived with a wagon carrying six hundred pounds of candy and personally handed it out to the camp's children.[86]

The Red Cross workers tried to provide the best food possible, and in fact, the refugees in 1927 fared much better than those fourteen years earlier. Refugees at "Camp Crump" in 1913 received salt meat, molasses, corn meal, sugar, coffee and flour. In 1927, refugees received lean salt meat, syrup, cream meal, sugar, coffee, self-rising flour, pork and beans, evaporated apples, prunes, salmon, black-eyed peas, salt, pepper, baking powder, canned turnip greens, evaporated milk, rice, canned tomatoes, potatoes, onions and canned sweet potatoes. They also received candles, matches, soap and laundry detergent. George Pratt, Red Cross food dispenser, said, "While not every one of the delicacies in the list was included in all rations, they were distributed as generously as our funds allowed."[87]

Refugees outside the fairgrounds often fell victim to the unsympathetic and unscrupulous. Toll collectors at the Harahan Bridge continued to charge fees until Crittenden County judge Renfro Turner ordered them to stop on April 21. Thieves stole the wagon, mules, cow and calf of an African American refugee from Marion, Arkansas, while he nursed his two sick children at the home of a relative at Iowa Avenue and Delaware Street. Some refugees turned down offers of assistance because of stories circulated in Memphis that Red Cross officials required refugees to sign an agreement to pay for material assistance. Mrs. John T. Fisher, supervisor of relief work at the auditorium, assured the public that flood victims only needed documentation from Lavinia Riley at the Red Cross headquarters to verify their refugee status and receive assistance.[88]

Hoover wanted the refugees out of the camps and back on their farms as soon as possible. However, farmers feared that the next round of seasonal flooding would ruin any new crops because of the lack of flood protection. Hoover ordered the broken levees closed before the "June rise," the seasonal flooding that typically occurred at the end of spring. Major General Edwin Jadwin of the Army Corps of Engineers assigned Colonel George Potter, chairman of the Mississippi River Commission, with the task of repairing the levees. Hoover hoped to encourage farmers to quickly begin replanting by convincing them the repaired levees would protect their farms.[89]

Mid-South refugee camps began to close as the flood crest passed. On May 14, the Red Cross ordered the Hickman, Kentucky refugee camp closed, while the headquarters remained open under the supervision of Lewis H. Kilpatrick. Camp officials provided transportation, and those without work received financial aid for two weeks. Refugees left the camp in Ripley, Tennessee, and returned to their farms in Lauderdale County in hopes of planting cotton before the season ended. Refugees from the camp in Belzoni, Mississippi, began returning home by the first week of May. Most of the refugee camps in Arkansas closed by the end of the month, as flood victims hurried home to try to plant crops. The remaining camps had only small numbers of people, left destitute and homeless.[90]

Clearing the camp in Memphis took several weeks. Camp officials allowed some of the fairgrounds refugees from Arkansas to begin checking out during the first week of May. As they left, others from farther south took their places. On May 5, the camp still held 1,365 refugees, and officials expected 17 more flood victims from Louisiana to arrive aboard the *Ossinger* from Vicksburg. Truckloads of workhouse prisoners arrived at the fairgrounds on May 13 to assist departing refugees, and Shelby County Commission chairman

Major General Edwin Jadwin. *Courtesy of Library of Congress.*

E.W. Hale promised to make the trucks and prisoners available as long as the disaster committee needed them. Camp officials cleared out the last of the refugees by May 20, and the fairgrounds reopened to the public with a celebration featuring a pageant, music and concessions on May 28. The swimming pool opened to the public at one o'clock, followed by concessions two hours later. The celebration included performances by the girls' drum corps, ukulele class, advanced dance class, a twenty-piece professional band and a performance of *Hansel and Gretel*.[91]

The camp gave city officials exactly what they wanted—it allowed them to simultaneously care for the refugees and keep them confined and closely monitored by the police. It served the city well in 1913 and 1927, and it would do so again in 1932 as a camp for Bonus Marchers headed for Washington, D.C. Like its counterparts in Arkansas and Mississippi, the Memphis camp kept its occupants in a controlled environment not very different from a prison camp. Camp officials provided mandatory inoculations to prevent outbreaks of disease that could threaten the city. They also provided food and entertainment to keep the refugees pacified while they waited to return to their plantations. Memphians kept up with the near-chaotic situations in other parts of the Mid-South—and they did not want the same in their city. The mayor and police department certainly did not want a situation in Memphis like that in other Mid-South communities, where mobs of refugees wandered the streets frightening citizens. In hindsight, one can see the harshness of the measures taken, but at the time, city officials considered their actions necessary to maintain order.[92]

Caring for those who traveled to Memphis proved a tremendous challenge, but the humanitarian effort did not end with them. Many others became trapped by floodwaters before they could escape. These unfortunate people took refuge on tiny scraps of land, in trees or on roofs, clinging to loved ones and possessions and praying for rescue.

Chapter 4
WATER, LAND AND AIR

When it thunders and lightnin' and when the wind begins to blow
When it thunders and lightnin' and the wind begins to blow
There's thousands of people ain't got no place to go
—Bessie Smith, "Backwater Blues"

Thunderstorms pounded the Mid-South as the crew of the steamer *Mary Frances* prepared for another rescue mission into Arkansas on April 25. The weather and a river stage reaching forty-six feet would make the journey especially dangerous. Pilots Frank Smith and Mr. Fogelson teamed with volunteers from the YMCA, including commander Sam Jackson and lifeguards Carol Walden, Ed Hutchinson, Henry Michael, Frank Leftwich, Harold Gillespie and Joe Hooper. They left the landing at Memphis at 8:00 a.m., fighting rough headwaters on the Mississippi River as they headed for the mouth of the St. Francis River. They reached the tributary at 2:00 p.m., making slow progress against the heavy current until they reached the levee break at Whitehall and stopped for the night.[93]

The rain continued as they set out the next morning at dawn in search of stranded flood victims. The crew of the *Mary Frances*, like other rescue crews, typically sailed into flooded areas and began blowing the steamer's whistle to make their presence known. Those with boats rowed out to the steamer, while the crew used johnboats to search for those stranded in their homes. Jackson and the others took on twelve refugees at Widener before continuing west to Madison, where they landed at 12:30 p.m. They received orders to proceed to Black Fish Bayou to evacuate more refugees, but the refugees in Madison desperately needed shelter. Jackson decided to leave for Forrest City to request additional tents and equipment for Madison, leaving the rest of the crew to continue on their journey.[94]

The rains had cleared by the time the *Mary Frances* reached the mouth of the Black Fish River at 2:30 p.m. At 6:30 pm, the boat landed at Walker's Place Plantation, where the crew found the remaining inhabitants marooned on mounds, in attics and in barn lofts. The thirty-five people taken aboard spent a miserable night on the deck, with temperatures in the low sixties and not enough blankets to go around.

The *Mary Frances* continued the next morning, taking on twelve more refugees at 9:30 a.m. and another four just three hours later. One seriously ill refugee, thirty-three-year-old Ellic Burton, died that afternoon. The boat landed at Rawlinson at 1:45 p.m. and took on thirty-seven refugees and eighteen more at Fred Edwards's plantation, where one of the women had just given birth.[95]

At 5:00 p.m., the crew attempted to cross a flooded field, only to run aground, delaying the trip for over an hour. The *Mary Frances* eventually rendezvoused with a couple of barges on which the refugees were able to eat and rest for the night. An African American man fell from one of the barges, but fortunately Ed Hutchinson dove in and saved him. The expedition returned to Madison, and the refugees received transportation to a Red Cross camp at Forrest City the next morning. The crew, including Sam Jackson, returned to Memphis by way of the St. Francis River the next morning to receive additional orders for their next rescue mission.[96]

Rescuers utilized every means available to provide assistance to flood victims in what became the largest disaster relief operation in U.S. history. Boats, trains, aircraft and radio played important roles in operations. However, the courage of the men and women who risked their lives to save total strangers—more than anything else—determined the outcome of the disaster.

The Midwest branch office of the Red Cross in St. Louis urged refugees to remain in their districts whenever possible and restricted W.B. Bayless, chairman of the Memphis Red Cross chapter, to supervise relief work in Shelby and Tipton Counties only. The Army Corps of Engineers, on the other hand, immediately sent boats, barges and crews for rescue work in Arkansas. Engineer William Parkin supervised the rescue and transfer of refugees to the National Guard camp at Marianna. Major Godfrey of the U.S. Dredge Fleet turned over the *Choctaw* and the *Mercury*, each with crews

Steamer *Inspector* at Helena, Arkansas, April 23, 1927. *Courtesy of Library of Congress.*

of thirty, to Major Donald Connolly for rescue operations and sent another twenty men to help direct crews in New Orleans.[97]

Connolly stayed on the job continuously, only snatching naps during brief lulls in his office next to a map used to track the flood. The red-eyed engineer maintained telephone and radio contact with communities throughout the flooded areas. His office's telephones rang incessantly with calls from isolated stations reporting the conditions of levees, the need for supplies or requests to rescue flood victims marooned on Indian mounds, hills or levees. Connolly also made frequent personal inspections of the levees by airplane and boat. The forty-one-year-old Arizona native did not shy away from responsibilities or challenges. He attended the University of California, received a commission in the Army Corps of Engineers from West Point in 1910 and graduated from the Army War College in 1923. Later, he would work at the War College, the WPA and the Civil Aeronautics Department before his promotion to brigadier general in 1941. He would serve during World War II and act as the postwar army commander in Iran and Iraq.[98]

Major General Edwin Jadwin centralized operations by having Connolly handle all requests for supplies and ordering representatives from the Fourth, Fifth, Sixth and Seventh Army Corps to report to Memphis to coordinate rescue operations. On April 21, officers of the Third and Fourth Army Corps arrived first and set up a central base for relief operations on the tenth floor of the McCall Building. Connolly's office handled telephone calls and provided maps, while Major D.C.T. Grubbs of the Seventh Army Corps of Omaha, Nebraska, directed activities in Arkansas and Missouri; Captain Francis Maslin of the Fifth Army Corps directed activities in Tennessee, Mississippi and Louisiana; and Major Gordon H. McCoy assisted as executive officer.[99]

Rescuers commandeered various private and government boats for work in Arkansas and Mississippi. Crews worked to the point of exhaustion, traveling hundreds of miles throughout the day and into the night. The U.S. Army Corps of Engineers' dredge boat *Choctaw* left on April 21 for the vicinity of Reydel and Waldstein, bringing food and supplies to over two hundred Arkansans marooned after the levee near England failed. The Tennessee Hoop Company's towboat *Tennessee*, along with the *Mary Frances* and other vessels, traveled up and down the St. Francis and Arkansas Rivers carrying supplies and refugees to Forrest City on April 23. The *Tennessee* returned from rescue work in Arkansas and left again for Greenville, Mississippi, carrying gasoline, two tons of potatoes, over eight thousand loaves of bread, five-gallon containers of drinking water, several tons of other food and supplies and three telegraph operators to restore communications.[100]

Radio and telephone played a larger role in relief efforts than ever before. Red Cross director Henry Baker made use of commercial and military radio to coordinate evacuations and relief operations, which in turn enabled workers in remote camps to request assistance and supplies from Memphis. Each home and business with a radio became a gathering place to listen to the latest updates from WMC, the station of the *Commercial Appeal* and *Evening Appeal*. Stores, such as Wilenzick's in Augusta, Arkansas, transcribed and posted every bulletin in their front windows. Local telephones quickly became bogged down. Frank Flournoy, general manager of the Southern Bell Telephone and Telegraph Company, asked that Memphians limit telephone calls to flooded areas since "curiosity calls" overtaxed the operators' equipment and hindered emergency communications. Baker requested twelve radio units from the U.S. Army on April 26 to expand the communications network in the Mississippi Valley to include the most isolated communities. He established Memphis as the central signal station and used airplanes and boats to locate the other units in the flooded areas.[101]

Colonel George R. Spalding of the Army Corps of Engineers arrived from Louisville, Kentucky, on April 26 to take charge of all water transportation

Steamer *Kate Adams* at Memphis, April 22, 1927. *Courtesy of Library of Congress.*

and rescue work. Within hours of his arrival, his staff assembled a fleet from every available government vessel and private boat, marking the first time in history that all watercraft in the Mississippi Valley fell under the control of one person. He instructed all commercial operators to report to his office every day between 6:00 p.m. and midnight for instructions for rescue and relief operations. Various companies provided vessels: the Standard Oil Company of Louisiana turned over all water facilities and two boats; the Ohio River Valley Improvement Association contributed the steamers *John Barrett*, *Patricia Barrett* and *Dorothy Barrett*; and the *Newport News* (Virginia) offered fifteen lifeboats. West Kentucky Coal Company's *Oleando* and the Army Corps of Engineers' *Tuscombia* and *Guyandot* from St. Louis received modifications to allow them to act as mother ships for smaller craft.[102]

Soon, Spalding needed more boats to keep up with hundreds of requests via airplane, radio, telegraph, telephone and messenger to rescue flood victims. Baker telegraphed Treasury secretary Andrew Mellon on the night of April 26 and requested one hundred more U.S. Coast Guard watercraft as soon as possible. Various vessels soon arrived from different parts of the country. Superintendent B.W. Southgate of the Cincinnati Lighthouse District dispatched two lighthouse tender boats, *Wake Robin* and *Greenbriar,* to Memphis to accompany the government towboats *Cayuga, Iroquois, Ottawa* and *Kentucky*, which were already en route. The *Tallapoosa*, *Shawnee* and *Pawnee* joined the fleet, which included six seventy-five-foot ships and hundreds of smaller vessels. However, even with the additional vessels Spalding could not keep up with the requests for help from Arkansas. On April 29, Baker requested another hundred more boats from Lake Huron, Lake Michigan, Lake Erie and the Gulf of Mexico.[103]

The rescue fleet followed the crest as it slowly moved toward New Orleans, navigating tributaries, inspecting levees, moving supplies and transporting refugees. On May 3, Spalding sent the *John Barrett* and *Dorothy Barrett*, *Guyandot*, *Iroquois*, *Cayuga*, *Choctaw*, *Tuscumbia* and *Augustine* to the area between Natchez and Vicksburg to join forces with ten other steamers and five seventy-five-foot U.S. Coast Guard chasers. The steamers *Control*, *Wabash*, *Tollinger* and *Louisville* provided assistance to refugees along the Yazoo River, while *Ranshall*, *C.J. Miller*, *Vicksburg*, *Panther*, *Yocona*, *Badger*, *Otter*, *Tin Pan*, *Chuckle*, *Hamlet*, *Tallulah* and *Kankakee* worked along the Yazoo and Sunflower Rivers. The U.S. Coast Guard vessel *Kankakee* left Memphis on April 26 for Greenville and Helena with supplies and a fire engine. It also acted as a mother ship for smaller boats and skiffs used to rescue those marooned by the flood. The crew of the *Kankakee* had rescued over one thousand people from rooftops and trees so far, transporting over six hundred in one night on April 23.[104]

Barge loaded with refugees arriving at Helena, Arkansas. *Courtesy of Library of Congress.*

Baker acknowledged the enormity of the disaster in the Mississippi Valley but felt the Red Cross had made progress in providing aid to refugees. He stated, "The emergency situation is gradually being brought under control and reports last night from our workers in almost every flood section were to the effect that supplies of food, tents, and other essentials were moving forward satisfactorily." The Red Cross transported tons of items to area refugee camps over the next two days—crews sent 1,550 tents from St. Louis to Helena; the Lee Lumber Company of Memphis sent twenty-five skiffs built by volunteers to Cleveland, Mississippi; and the Red Cross shipped a rail car full of sweet potatoes donated by farmers in Paris, Tennessee, to the refugee camp in Wynne. The crew of the *Kankakee* delivered 200 tents, one thousand blankets and stoves for refugees stranded on levees in Arkansas City. The ship's commander, John Hill of Denver, Colorado, then transported all the white women and children to Rosedale, Mississippi, where they boarded a train for Cleveland, Mississippi.[105]

Mississippi levee officials made a plea through the *Commercial Appeal* for riverboats to immediately evacuate residents following the break at Scott's Landing. On April 22, Dr. Louis Leroy, along with Thornton Newsum and Henry R. Colby, led a small flotilla of four motorboats with food, supplies and two hundred copies of the *Memphis Evening Appeal* to Greenville following a massive levee break. Leroy had many accomplishments, including a career as a prominent pathologist, physician and a medical expert in legal proceedings. He installed Memphis's first X-ray machine, drove the first automobile in Tennessee and once played World Chess champion Emanuel Lasker to a draw. Leroy also had an almost mythical reputation as a boat pilot and river sportsman, in part from helping passengers rescued by Tom Lee when the *Norman* sank near Memphis in 1925.[106]

Leroy and his team of volunteers assisted in rescue and relief efforts in Mississippi and Arkansas with a "fleet of mercy speedboats" consisting of the *50-50*; the *Sunshine*, owned by James Canale of D. Canale and Company; the *Mark Twain*, owned by the estate of the late Russell Martin; and the *Navajo*, owned by Winston Carter. On one occasion, Leroy encountered a crew that had used an airplane engine and propeller to power an old scow. The contraption worked well until it ran out of gas, leaving the crew adrift. Fortunately, Leroy spotted them when they used a flashlight to signal for help. A mother who climbed a telephone pole with her two small children held on for thirty-six hours before Leroy and his crew spotted her. They had to pry her cramped and swollen hands from the children. Once freed, the

Speedboat on rescue mission. *Author's collection.*

exhausted mother fell into the water and nearly drowned before rescuers pulled her into the boat.[107]

While in Greenville, the mercy speedboat crews rescued at least two hundred people and established a ferry to carry the sick to area hospitals and refugee camps. Leroy helped medical authorities as well, assisting with the vaccinations of over four thousand refugees while Jim Canale led *Sunshine*, *Mark Twain* and *Navaho* to Arkansas City on April 29. Leroy said, "Many lives have been lost; there's no question about that. I count it conservative indeed to estimate the dead at around one hundred and fifty. Numbers of bodies are being recovered now and the receding waters will uncover more. We buried seventeen at one time."[108]

The rescuers risked their lives many times during the two weeks spent in Mississippi. They faced many hazards, from crossing twisted railway lines to avoiding fallen electrical wires. During one unfortunate incident, one of the crew had to have an arm amputated after he came in contact with a high-tension wire. Even their trip home presented dangers. They left Greenville on May 3, and three days later they had to avoid a tornado near Cat Island,

Refugees line up for vaccinations in Greenville, Mississippi. *Courtesy of Library of Congress.*

opposite Tunica Landing. The exhausted volunteers finally returned to Memphis on the evening of May 6.[109]

One incident on the night of April 21 further illustrates the dangers faced by those who worked on the Mississippi River during the flood. Eighteen workers waited aboard the government launch *Pelican* for transfer to the steamer *Wabash* at Knowlton's Point in Desha County, Arkansas. During the high winds, heavy rain and hail, the nearby levee suddenly collapsed and the river burst through the gap, carrying the *Pelican* along. The launch twisted, spun and sank within seconds.[110]

Those aboard the approaching *Wabash* watched in horror as the *Pelican* tumbled through the levee break. The big steamer had to keep its distance from the crevasse or risk the same fate as the launch. However, Sam Tucker, an African American member of the crew, decided to take matters into his own hands. He single-handedly piloted a skiff through the torrent in hopes of saving the *Pelican's* crew. He braved the elements and guided the unpowered vessel through the debris, unwilling to give up on the unfortunate rivermen. Tucker found the only survivors, two men who jumped overboard. He pulled the exhausted men into the tiny boat and rowed upstream back to the *Wabash*.[111]

C.L. Morris, an employee of the R.T. Clark Construction Company, witnessed the sinking. He found a boat and crossed the river to Perthshire, Mississippi, where he telephoned Arthur Wells of Helena and told him about the wreck. At the time, Morris believed that no one had survived. Wells passed along the information, and the Red Cross at Memphis dispatched the steamer *Chisca* to investigate and search for more survivors.[112]

Residents of Knowlton's Point quickly evacuated as the floodwaters swept through their community. The wife of levee engineer John Stansell, who left for Memphis to stay with her sister, informed the *Evening Appeal* that everyone had fled the community by April 22. Floodwaters washed away houses and barns in low-lying areas, leaving nothing more than foundations. Evacuations spread planters' tenants and livestock around to various refugee camps. The levee break left the area so devastated that planter Abe Knowlton, who also fled to Memphis, believed that even if the waters receded by June 1 farmers still would not make a crop.[113]

The *Commercial Appeal* began a campaign to raise money for the widows and orphans of Memphis crewmen lost on the *Pelican*. Reporters instructed readers to send money and clothing either to the newspaper office or directly to the widows at 206 Market Street. Sympathetic Memphians gave nearly $400 within a week after seeing the picture of the widowed Pearl Douglas with her children, Louise, Thomas and Denver, and Clara Hicks with her children, Hazel, Herman and Luther. The money raised helped the families while Joseph H. Henderson, special agent of the United States Employees' Compensation Commission, settled their claims. Henderson worked from the U.S. Army Corps of Engineers office at the McCall Building, where he prepared paperwork necessary to provide a monthly allowance to the families.[114]

Recovery of the bodies proved especially difficult because floodwaters carried the *Pelican* over a mile from the levee break. Rescue workers recovered the first four bodies on May 2 and seven more on May 3. The engineers could identify only three because of advanced decomposition, so they buried three unidentified African Americans and one white man in Rosedale.[115]

Sisters Pearl Douglas and Clara Hicks traveled to Rosedale on May 5 to recover the bodies of their husbands. They found Joe Hicks, but they could not make out Douglas's body. By May 13, relatives could identify only eleven of the twenty-five bodies: H.N. Owen, Oscar Craig, Henry Cooper, John White, W.B. Morris, Thomas Edward Sawner, Raymond Burleson, Charles Craig, Charles Henry, Ernest Neal and Resse Brown. White and Sawner were interred in Elmwood Cemetery, Cooper was laid to rest in Memphis

Memorial Park on May 7 and Morris was laid to rest in Forest Hill Cemetery two days later. The U.S. Army Corps of Engineers transferred the others to their respective hometowns.[116]

A.T. Stovall Jr., general agent for the Columbus and Greenville Railroad, sat in the Peabody Hotel in Memphis, where he described for a reporter "the wildest night" of his life. He had just left Greenville when an eight-foot wave of water from the levee break slammed into his freight train. The water immediately put out the engine fire, leaving the train and its crew stranded. The water rose so high that the crew had to climb to the top of the boxcars. As they waited, fifteen more people from nearby farms caught by floodwaters washed up to the train. The crew caught the farmers and helped them climb out of the water. They waited through the "long horror" for rescue, fearing a second wave of water might completely submerge the train. Stovall said, "It will be sometime before we can recover the engine and cars from their position and must wait until the water recedes. I made a trip down there in a motor boat and no one can begin to compute the damage Greenville has suffered."[117]

On April 20, at 1:30 a.m., floodwaters burst through the St. John's Bayou levee, covering New Madrid with one to five feet of water. The levee ruptured again the next day, sending a stream of water several miles wide toward Arkansas. J.E. Hutchinson, vice-president and general manager of the Frisco Railroad, left Memphis for Lilbourn, Missouri, to monitor rail lines following a second levee break. However, he could only watch as the rush of water swept away railbeds and twisted rails beyond recognition.[118]

The flood crippled the railroads in the Mississippi Valley. Floodwaters swept through the Delta with such force that they often tore tracks off their railbeds, making them stand on their sides and giving the appearance of picket fences. Repairs exceeded $10 million and brought transportation, one of Memphis's principal industries, almost to a halt. Floodwaters had either slowed or detoured rail service from Memphis to Cape Girardeau and throughout eastern Arkansas by April 18. The 8:00 a.m. St. Louis Express had to stop and turn back, and the Kansas City–Florida Special from Black Rock, Arkansas, arrived forty-five minutes late in Memphis because of water covering the tracks. Over three hundred yards of Rock Island Railroad tracks washed out near Biscoe, Arkansas, the next day. This forced the railroad to reroute the only remaining connection from Memphis to the Southwest over the Cotton Belt line via Brinkley and Stuttgart.[119]

Flooding all but shut down rail service to and from Memphis after April 20. Memphians hung flags along Main Street in anticipation of the annual

Railroad tracks washed out near Memphis. *Author's collection.*

A boxcar falls into floodwater after part of the railroad tracks were washed away. *Author's collection.*

convention of the sixteenth district Rotarians, but Larry S. Akers, rotary district manager, cancelled the event because trains could not bring the conventioneers to the city. Floodwaters isolated Little Rock after officials suspended rail service because of submerged tracks. Water from a break in the St. Francis levee struck the Cotton Belt Railway Bridge near Paragould with such force that it pushed the pilings out of alignment, suspending rail service until crews made repairs. Floodwaters near Hughes caused rails to shift and spread, stranding a Missouri Pacific train carrying refugees bound for Memphis. As many as two hundred people abandoned the train and returned by motorboat to flood-ravaged Hughes rather than risking a possible derailment.[120]

The Interstate Commerce Commission declared a transportation emergency and ordered that railroads in flooded areas suspend normal operations and focus on transporting refugees to safety. On April 20, the Missouri Pacific Railroad moved four hundred boxcars of refugees out of flooded areas in eastern Arkansas to camps in western Arkansas and Memphis. Another twenty boxcars carried between five hundred and one thousand refugees from the lower St. Francis Basin on the Missouri Pacific Railroad to Memphis, stopping briefly at Chatfield because of flooded tracks. A crew of cooks and waiters traveled from Memphis to Brinkley to run kitchens set up by the dining car service on the Cotton Belt Route for those waiting for transportation to Red Cross camps. Railroads in Memphis, Birmingham, Atlanta and New Orleans donated twenty-four Pullman cars for use in Vicksburg. Each car came with porters and space for twenty-eight people, and an additional kitchen car could accommodate fifty-four people.[121]

Normal operations resumed as the floodwaters began to recede, though parts of Mississippi remained under water until summer. Rail service from Memphis opened to St. Louis and Kansas City on April 28, and by May 5, all railroads out of Memphis, except for Y&MV, had restored services to most areas in Arkansas. The Missouri Pacific Railroad restored service to Helena by May 15, and the Y&MV resumed service between Memphis and Greenville in early June. Even so, travel remained hazardous for months because of weakened railbeds and bridges. On July 28, a train carrying Vice President Charles Dawes from an American Legion convention in Greenville derailed near Head, Mississippi. Fortunately, most of the slow-moving train remained on the tracks, but the engine fell into forty-two feet of water, killing engineer Sam Jones of Memphis.[122]

Railroad workers frequently risked their lives in order to keep trains loaded with supplies and refugees moving. Smaller trains preceded passenger trains, making sure the tracks could support the heavier transports, while men perched on the fronts of the engines scanning for debris that could derail the train. Others in boats or in hip boots waded through the water at night, waving engineers along flooded tracks and keeping careful watch on weakening embankments and bridges and repaired twisted rails. They dove under water to throw submerged switches, drove trains over miles of flooded tracks and sandbagged embankments in order to keep lines of communication open.[123]

Friday the thirteenth lived up to its reputation as an unlucky day for Italian flyer Colonel Francesco de Pinedo, copilot Carlo del Prete and mechanical troubleshooter Sergeant Vitale Zacchetti. Radiator problems caused the flyers to have to make an emergency landing near Memphis while in the middle of a tour of the Americas following their historic transatlantic flight. De Pinedo mistook an overflow area for the Mississippi River and landed his amphibious Savoia-Marchetti S.55, *Santa Maria II*, near a sandbar two or three miles from the U.S. Navy airport. The plane drifted inland, where a U.S. launch found him and brought him to Memphis.[124]

The radiator leak kept de Pinedo from continuing his flight to Chicago, much to his annoyance, and forced him to have to deal with local well-wishers. Stranded until May 16, the weary Italian made the best of the situation. Mayor Paine, Senator Kenneth McKellar, Colonel Waring, Watkins Overton and other city officials welcomed the ace. Hundreds of Italian Americans and other Memphians rushed to the waterfront to greet him, including Detective Sergeant Mario Chiozza; Ulbaldo Andreucetti, editor of the local Italian-language newspaper; Captain del Prete, a native of the flyer's hometown, Lucca; and former Italian consul John Galella. The current Italian consul in Memphis, John Di Gaetani, suggested a banquet in honor of the "Ace of Aces," but the Spartan flyer, running out of patience, refused, saying, "No, I don't like them [banquets]. I have business to attend to. Four minutes is long enough for any man to eat a meal."[125]

The public had a great deal of interest in reports from flyers traveling over the flood area. Newspapermen asked about what the pilot saw as he traveled across the Mississippi Valley. De Pinedo offered his sympathies for the flood victims: "I saw houses floating away this morning. I felt sorry for the people. The flood is a great disaster. We were flying too high to see much of the country, but we saw water enough to realize the enormity of the flood."[126]

Aviators kept lines of communication open through the worst of the flood, and their efforts helped pave the way for Memphis to become an important aviation center. Pilots such as Vernon and Phoebe Omilie made numerous flights carrying mail, medicine, newspapers and correspondence between Little Rock, Batesville, Pine Bluff, Conway and Memphis after floodwaters washed out bridges, highways and railroads, isolating most of central and western Arkansas. News services such as the Associated Press and *National Geographic* toured flood zones by air, gathered information and kept the outside world informed about the disaster.

Vernon and Phoebe Omile. *Courtesy of the Memphis and Shelby County Room, Memphis Public Library and Information Center.*

Memphis newspapers the *Commercial Appeal* and *Memphis Evening Appeal* continued deliveries throughout the Mid-South with aircraft, providing the latest news about flooding and evacuations.[127]

Thirty planes surveyed the disaster area twice each day, patrolling a four-hundred-mile area south of Memphis into Arkansas and Mississippi.

An amphibious navy airplane lands next to the flooded Mud Island. *Courtesy of Library of Congress.*

Unable to land, they could do little more than report the whereabouts of survivors and occasionally drop supplies of typhoid serum and sandwiches to medical staff and refugees on the levees and rooftops. Near England, Arkansas, an airplane observer saw a shirt waving from a hole in the roof of a cotton gin. The pilot returned daily for the next ten days, "bombing" the hole accurately with supplies and saving the refugees' lives. Major Donald Connolly and other engineers used a standard land-based plane at first to inspect levees in the district but had difficulty finding suitable places to land. Connolly made a request for an amphibious airplane on April 18 that allowed him to land on water and make more careful examinations of flood works. More of these aircraft soon followed, allowing easier access to levees and stranded refugees.[128]

Henry Baker had already conscripted every available water vessel, and now he wanted to add to his growing fleet of aircraft. Seaplanes from Pensacola arrived on April 26 for the Red Cross in Memphis, Lake Village, Vicksburg and New Orleans for use in delivering supplies to stranded refugees and surveying flooded areas. Baker requested six additional amphibious airplanes from the navy that evening. Lieutenants J.G. Farrell and J.E. Beck left Pensacola at 2:00 p.m. for New Orleans and then made the six-hour trip to Memphis with the first two planes. Baker had eleven seaplanes at various locations in the Mid-South under his command by April 28. By May 5, he

U.S. Navy seaplanes gather near Confederate Park in Memphis. *Courtesy of Library of Congress.*

had nearly fifty aircraft at his disposal for rescue and relief operations, as well as planes from Dayton, Ohio, equipped to photograph the progress of the flood.[129]

Bry's Department Store manager Ed Saloman, who sold airplanes to the growing numbers of flying enthusiasts in the Mid-South, donated airplanes for rescue work as well. Saloman offered Hoover and his assistants the use of his store's new Eaglerock biplane, along with the services of pilot Lieutenant Windham. The store's staff dismantled the display airplane, reassembled it at the flying field for use in flood service and requested more planes from Bry's St. Louis factory.[130]

Not surprisingly, Bry's helped lead the way in expanding aviation in Memphis. On May 8, the store opened a 268-acre airport five miles east of Memphis on Raleigh Road to improve airmail service. It included towers and hangars for four Eaglerock airplanes, as well as a playground and baseball diamond. Ed Salomon presided at the opening of the festivities with Mayor Payne in attendance. Pilots offered rides in an Eaglerock airplane that had a camera, allowing the passenger to take a self-portrait in the air with the city in the background.[131]

Airplane dealers found many local customers, and commercial aviation steadily grew. An editorial author wrote that Memphians "are becoming aviation-minded," as evidenced by the establishment of airmail service between Memphis and Little Rock. He accurately predicted the establishment of a permanent National Guard air unit and the creation of an airport to equal the river port, railway terminals and highways that made Memphis an important distribution center. Memphis had the highest concentration of airfields anywhere in the region, but the growing air traffic—especially witnessed during the flood—illustrated the need for a larger and better equipped municipal airport.[132]

P.D. Cramer and D.R. Scarritt from the commerce department spoke on April 26 at the Peabody Hotel about Memphis's need for an airport. The two came to town because of the regulations passed the previous year that required the commerce department to inspect aircraft and check pilots' licenses annually. They inspected five aircraft and examined Vernon and Phoebe Omilie, John Barron, Chatham and Manuel Hunter and Hubert Gay. Cramer said:

> Memphis should by all means establish an airport and encourage aviation commercially...a colony of active aviators would be a prime factor in the business life of Memphis. What a tremendous advantage and benefit during and previous to the present big flood a battery of flyers would have been to the Mississippi Valley had Memphis had an airport with a colony of aviators the world can now see. Lives could have been saved, possibly levee breaks anticipated by inspection and prevented.[133]

Aviation helped the Army Corps of Engineers and the Red Cross during the flood, but not without its fair share of danger. Air operations proved almost as hazardous relief as work on the rivers on a number of occasions. Major Connolly's first amphibious plane due in from Langley, Virginia, crashed at Louisville, Kentucky, on its way to Memphis. Fortunately, the pilot, Lieutenant Hiller, and his mechanic escaped without serious injury. A storm forced pilot Lieutenant Vernon Omilie to make an emergency landing at Hazen, Arkansas, while delivering mail to Little Rock. Two planes carrying medical supplies into Mississippi made emergency landings east of Vicksburg on May 4. Unable to take off again, the pilots unloaded their supplies to trucks that delivered them to Delhi.[134]

The most tragic accident involved Red Cross assistant director Earl Kilpatrick, who supervised rehabilitation in the Mid-South following the relocation of the Red Cross headquarters from Memphis to New Orleans. He planned to meet with Henry Baker at the new headquarters for about three hours and return to Memphis by the evening of May 30. However, during the flight out of Memphis, pilot Lieutenant Joe Gregory suddenly lost control of the plane about forty miles south of Baton Rouge. He said that it "slipped from under him" and went into a nosedive, crashing in a field in Hohen. Gregory survived, but Kilpatrick died instantly. Gregory went to New Orleans by car, while Kilpatrick's body remained for examination by the local coroner before being returned to his hometown of Webster Grove, Missouri.[135]

Modern technology provided rescuers advantages not previously available in earlier flood relief efforts: motorboats aided the evacuations, trains carried people to shelters on high ground, airplanes helped locate survivors clinging to rooftops or tree limbs and delivered communications and vital supplies and radios broadcast warnings to residents in the path of floodwaters. In addition, journalists used radios and photography to inform the world about the plight of people in the Mississippi Valley, which in turn shaped public opinion and forced government action. More importantly, technology helped relief crews who laid their lives on the line every day in hopes of saving just one more person from drowning, disease or starvation.

Chapter 5

COLOSSUS OF THE MISSISSIPPI FLOOD DISASTER

Said me and my good girl talked last night,
Me and her talked for hours
She wanted me to go to the Red Cross Store
And get a sack of that Red Cross flour
Say you know them Red Cross folks there,
They sure do treat you mean
Don't want to give you nothin'
But two-three cans of beans
—Walter Roland, "Red Cross Blues"[136]

On the morning of April 25, Mayor Paine waited at the station for the train from Washington carrying President Coolidge's representatives. Three days earlier, the president, who also served as president of the Red Cross, had accepted Paine's offer to use Memphis as the site of the agency's headquarters. Memphis, because of its resources, location on high ground and access to transportation, proved the logical choice. Coolidge appointed Secretary of Commerce Herbert Hoover to head relief operations and provided him with a committee that included Major General Edwin Jadwin of the U.S. Army Corps of Engineers, Red Cross chairman James L. Fieser and Henry M. Baker. With the help of Red Cross financial representative Frank A. Ellithorp, the committee was to oversee distribution of supplies and aid to flood victims.[137]

The Memphis Chamber of Commerce provided space to Hoover for relief operations on the third floor of their building. On April 23, executive director

C.M. Anderson and his staff set up a private office for Baker, with a larger adjoining area for his immediate staff. Anderson's staff put in telephones, a private switchboard, a workshop and a conference room, and they hung the Red Cross flag from one of the windows. [138]

The train carrying Hoover, Fieser, Baker and various reporters arrived Monday at 7:30 a.m. After brief introductions to the mayor, the stern-faced quartet posed for a newspaper photograph before heading to the Peabody Hotel. During a hurried breakfast, Hoover spoke with Paine and reporter Mark York about the situation in the flood zones and in the fairgrounds camp. The anxious Hoover checked his watch, asking, "What time is it? My watch is never right." York asked about the refugee problem.

Secretary of Commerce Herbert Hoover. *Courtesy of Library of Congress.*

"There are three things to be done for the flood victims," he said between mouthfuls of bacon and eggs. "First of all, we must get them out; second, we must feed them while they are out; third, and most serious of all, start them all over when the waters recede." He added with a smile, "The United States is certainly rich enough to do that, don't you think?" Hoover looked at his watch again and said, "I'm behind schedule." He asked Paine about the fairgrounds camp. The mayor told him about the refugees' pitiful efforts to save belongings, livestock and pets. Hoover commented as he put down his coffee cup, "There isn't much humor in the situation." Paine continued to discuss events in Greenville, Mississippi. After a pause, Hoover asked for the check, but Paine had already paid it. Hoover smiled and joked, "Now Mayor, you don't have to do that. I still make enough money to pay for what I eat and a place to sleep." As the men shared a laugh, the commerce secretary checked his watch again and said, "Way behind schedule. I've got to hustle and get on the job."[139]

Hoover, anxious to get busy, asked Paine for the names of people who could tell him more about the flood and the refugees. The mayor mentioned a twenty-six-year-old *Commercial Appeal* reporter by the name of Turner Catledge who had recently traveled to Cairo, Illinois; Columbus, Kentucky; and Greenville, Mississippi, covering the progress of the flood. Hoover insisted on meeting him, so Paine sent a couple of police detectives to Catledge's house on Eastmoreland Avenue.[140]

Soon after, the detectives were standing on his front porch, beating on the door. Catledge had flown back from Greenville the day before with Vernon Omlie, wrote a couple of stories for the paper and delivered a live report over WMC before falling into bed exhausted. Catledge's mother, who thought the police came to arrest him, woke him and rushed him to the door. The detectives assured her that they had not come to make an arrest but rather to ask for the young reporter's help. Catledge quickly dressed and rode with the detectives to the Peabody to meet with Hoover.[141]

At 9:30 a.m., Hoover held a two-hour conference at the Red Cross office at the chamber of commerce, where he commended the Red Cross for its efforts in organizing refugee camps. He outlined his plans for a central disaster relief headquarters with Henry Baker in charge and announced that Colonel George Spalding would act as liaison officer in charge of water transportation and rescue. Following the conference, Hoover accompanied Paine and Catledge to the fairgrounds camp, where he spoke with refugees about their immediate concerns and what they needed to rebuild after the flood.[142]

Afterward, Hoover returned to downtown Memphis to look at the flood as he waited to depart for Greenville. He stood on the banks of the Mississippi River and gazed across the sea of floodwater that extended for miles into Arkansas. He looked down at the water rushing by and told the *New York Times* reporter with him that two million cubic feet of water passed where they stood every minute. He asked his companion, "Do you realize what that means? It means that at this moment the volume of water passing Memphis is ten times greater than that pouring over the Niagara cliffs when the Niagara River is at maximum flood stage, and nearly three times that of the Colorado River when the floodwaters of that great stream are at

Floodwaters rising over cobblestones along the Memphis waterfront, April 23, 1927. *Courtesy of the Memphis and Shelby County Room, Memphis Public Library and Information Center.*

their absolute maximum peak." At two o'clock, Hoover and his entourage boarded the government steamer *Chisca* for Greenville and continued to Vicksburg before boarding a train for New Orleans.[143]

The people of the flood-stricken Mississippi Valley had high hopes that the "Great Humanitarian" would organize and speed up the arrival of badly needed help. Tired of inaction from the federal government, they wanted to see a man of action take the reins of the relief efforts. Hoover, with his experience and reputation as an effective leader, was the ideal choice to head relief and recovery operations. One writer called Hoover the "Colossus of the Mississippi Flood Disaster," while another writer described news of the arrival of Hoover, Fieser, Baker and Jadwin on April 25 as "celestial music to those who may hear the roaring of the flood about them."[144]

Hoover had served as a young engineer in Australia before becoming a mining director in China at the time of the Boxer Rebellion, during which he supervised relief efforts for besieged foreigners in Tientsin. The experience prepared him to lead the relief commission in Belgium and the food commission in the United States during World War I. President Wilson appointed him the head of the relief commission for Europe following the war, and in 1921, he mobilized private charities to help pay for grain seed for starving Russians in the Volga. Many in the Mississippi Valley wondered if his efforts would lead him to a higher office. An editorialist for the *Commercial Appeal* wrote, "Is it wondered that suggestions of Herbert Hoover as fine presidential timber are being echoed in the flooded southwest territory?"[145]

The concentration of a wide array of governmental powers in a single set of hands enabled the federal government to respond rapidly without bureaucratic impediments. James L. Fieser, vice-chairman of the Red Cross, directly assisted Hoover, while the remainder of the Mississippi River Valley Flood Commission—including the secretaries of the Departments of the Treasury, War and Navy and the members of the Red Cross Central Committee—served to provide expert advice and expedite resource provision. On April 22, the committee met for the first time and made three major decisions: first, it effectively turned over direction of the Red Cross's relief effort to Hoover; second, it appointed Henry Baker, disaster relief director for the Red Cross, as the actual administrator of the response effort who would work to execute Hoover's directions; and third, the commission agreed that each of the affected states should appoint a "dictator"—an individual who would serve as the point person to oversee the allocation of state resources.[146]

Hoover organized the efforts of the diverse relief organizations and toured the surrounding flooded areas, while Baker oversaw relief efforts from Memphis and coordinated the activities of the surrounding army districts. The headquarters housed operational units, including purchase and supply, river transportation and rescue work and rail transportation. Baker sat at the heart of the federal government and Red Cross partnership both figuratively and literally. Federal agency members, from the army to the public health service, and several governors sat near Baker's desk, where they could immediately respond to his requests. Thirty yards away, a Red Cross purchasing agent stood on a platform and shouted out supplies and quantities needed, and dozens of suppliers responded with bids.[147]

Baker's staff included Major Jesse Gaston, liaison officer with the Fourth, Fifth, Sixth and Seventh Army Corps; Foster M. Davis, Red Cross field representative for Indiana; Red Cross accountants J.A. Hendrix, J. Smith and I. McIntyre; and A.L. Schafer, assistant national director of the Junior Red Cross and liaison with Mississippi governor Dennis Murphree. Lieutenant W.D. Sample of the Pensacola naval base flew in by seaplane from Lake Village, Arkansas, to confer with Baker about bringing in additional aircraft. J.W. Richardson arrived the following day from the St. Louis Red Cross headquarters to act as the assistant to Baker. Colonel George Spalding supervised all water transportation and rescue work, and J.F. Porterfield, general manager of the Illinois Central Railroad, supervised all land transportation in the flooded areas.[148]

Hoover traveled to Mississippi to meet with William Percy, who served in Hoover's Commission for Relief in Belgium for two years during World War I, to inspect the flooded areas and to coordinate relief and rehabilitation efforts. The secretary arrived in Greenville early in the morning on April 25 and found a city under water and under military rule as a result of what reporters called the "restlessness" of the previous few days. The trouble began when Percy arranged to evacuate the African American plantation workers in order to provide them better care. Local planters wanted to keep the workers in local camps out of fear that they would not return. The landowners convinced Percy's father, Senator Leroy Percy, to change his son's mind. The younger Percy caved into the demands and cancelled the evacuation. He tried to justify the decision to his former commanding officer by saying that bringing supplies to the workers would prove easier than evacuation. Hoover turned a blind eye as the angry workers remained in forced labor camps for the duration of the flood. The event served as a sad reminder of African Americans' continued status as chattel in Mississippi.[149]

Hoover met with Governor Dennis Murphree of Mississippi at the wharf in Vicksburg on the afternoon of April 25. The two discussed plans for rebuilding the devastated areas in Mississippi with federal funding and remarked on the state's relief agency's efforts. An observer commented, "Mr. Hoover is not given to much excessive speech, but he used a great many words down here tonight complimenting the state forces." Hoover assigned a liaison officer who remained in constant contact with the Memphis headquarters with a special leased telephone wire.[150]

Hoover insisted that Turner Catledge accompany him to Greenville and remain with him as he traveled to Vicksburg and New Orleans. The reporter agreed and turned back the amphibious plane that arrived to return him to Memphis. Catledge advised Hoover and provided editorial assistance to the other reporters unfamiliar with the South. He also helped the journalists locate poker games, whiskey and female companionship. Hoover did not care for the reporters' recreational activities; however, the secretary liked Catledge so much that he wrote a letter to Adolph Ochs, publisher of the *New York Times*, recommending that Ochs hire the young writer.[151]

Catledge and Hoover left Greenville for Vicksburg at 8:45 a.m. aboard the *Chisca* and then traveled to New Orleans, where engineers planned to blast a nearby levee to save the city from the approaching flood crest. Catledge faced a problem since he needed to turn his story into the *Memphis Evening*

Appeal before the noon explosion, so he decided to write the story in advance in order to meet the deadline. He dramatically wrote, "With one thunderous roar, like the crack of doom, earth went flying heaven-ward, the City of New Orleans was relieved." Unfortunately, the gun-shy engineers used too few explosives, resulting in a "pop" rather than a "thunderous roar." It took another four days before workers with picks and shovels finally opened the crevasse. Embarrassed, Catledge had to write a correction for the following day's paper. Fortunately, the mistake did not hurt him too badly, and the *Baltimore Sun* hired him later that summer. Two years later, he took advantage of Hoover's recommendation and landed a position with the *New York Times*, where he worked his way up the ranks to become the paper's managing editor, executive editor and, eventually, vice-president.[152]

In Vicksburg, Hoover met again with Leroy Percy and his son, Will Percy. The Percys hoped that relief agencies would concentrate refugees near Vicksburg rather than evacuate them to Greenville. The Percys, like most Mississippi plantation owners, worried that their tenant farmers would not return after the evacuations—they wanted to keep them close to home. The Red Cross accommodated their wishes as much as possible, however, the widespread flooding often necessitated transport of flood victims away from their plantations. The steamers *Wabash, Sprague, Hunter, Ransdell, Tallulah* and *Charles J. Miller* continued to transport hundreds of refugees to Red Cross camps. By April 26, Vicksburg, Greenville, Cleveland and Yazoo City held a combined 7,931 refugees.[153]

Local law enforcement and the Red Cross officials made every effort to keep tenant farmers contained, leading to many complaints of abuse at the hands of camp officials. Hoover received near-absolute authority to merge federal resources, Red Cross volunteers and the private sector to carry out the relief and recovery program. This administrative structure may have removed unnecessary bureaucracy and clearly established Hoover's authority, but it had little direct effect on federal oversight of actual relief provision. This meant that Hoover could operate with few constraints and that local and state relief workers would not be held accountable when they broke the law.[154]

Hoover returned to Memphis, where he focused on the present problems of organizing relief efforts. On April 30, he met with a delegation of Arkansas leaders in Memphis: Governor John Martineau, Senator T.H. Caraway, Adjutant General J.R. Wayne, banker and University of Arkansas trustee Ernest Bodeman, Charles E. Thompson of the Little Rock Chamber of Commerce, Republican National Committee member Colonel H.L.

Steamer *Sprague* arriving at Vicksburg, Mississippi, with refugees. *Courtesy of Library of Congress.*

Remmel, Congressman W.J. Driver, engineer Colonel John R. Fordyce and Harvey Couch of the Arkansas Power and Light Company. Martineau appointed Couch as chairman of the relief committee after Hoover requested that he select a local leader to organize relief operations and determine the nature and extent of relief needed. Hoover also suggested that state banks approach northern banks about loans for rehabilitation. Congressman Whittington of Mississippi outlined the situation in his home state before Hoover concluded the conference. Hoover expressed sympathy for the residents of Arkansas and Mississippi and concluded the meeting by saying that he felt confident that Congress would approve money for aid to the flooded states.[155]

Before he left that evening for Washington, Hoover addressed the country from the WMC studio in the *Commercial Appeal* building. Speaking from downtown Memphis, just two blocks from the river, Hoover gave his assessment of the situation in the Mississippi Valley. He described the Mississippi River as the "gigantic spillway into the ocean for the waters of thirty states of the Midwest," whose rich flood plain attracted agricultural and urban development over the previous two centuries. He credited the levee system with acting as a great trough that contained seasonal floods, protecting homes and farms. He agreed with Jadwin that the answer to the flood problem lay in the need for higher levees and a southern spillway. He said, "In ordinary times these levees have been so successful that spring floods of the whole Midwest spill themselves peaceably into the gulf." He blamed the flood on the simultaneous spring rains over the Midwest, which caused floodwaters from a "dozen great rivers" to pass into the Mississippi River at once and overwhelm weaker parts of the levee system.[156]

Hoover explained why the U.S. Army Corps of Engineers continued to struggle to save the levees in the Mid-South rather than simply ordering complete evacuations of the flooded areas. He said, "We receive constant suggestions that all the people behind the threatened lines should be moved out in advance. But people do not and cannot surrender their crops, their cattle, their homes, until the battle is lost. We cannot order them to leave for we must not impose the suffering which is inseparable from abandonment of everything they hold dear." He stated that the engineers could divert the Mississippi River at New Orleans with a strategically placed cut in the levee, but the geography prevented them from using the same method in Arkansas and Mississippi. However, Hoover pointed out that rescue crews worked diligently to provide transportation, food, medical care and shelter to the thousands in Illinois, Kentucky, Tennessee, Arkansas, Mississippi and Louisiana forced to abandon their homes.[157]

Hoover praised the efforts of the people in the South and appealed to all Americans to contribute to the Red Cross effort to save the people of the Mississippi Valley from the "most dangerous flood our country has ever known." He said, "We the American people have created a great national organization that should ever be ready for great emergencies. The American Red Cross is that organization. And this, your organization is doing its duty effectively and efficiently. It is your hand carrying out the will of your great heart. It asks that you enlarge your support that it shall not fail."[158]

The Red Cross headquarters in Memphis certainly lived up to Hoover's expectations. It combined federal government, state governments, quasi-governmental entities, private citizens and businesses into a surprisingly smooth-running administrative machine with streams of coordinated responses known as "field operations letters" that were delivered by telephone, radio and messenger.[159] Hoover stated:

> At Memphis we have coordinated under the Red Cross, not only the personnel, equipment, and supplies of the federal departments, but also coordinated with local citizens, committees, Red Cross chapters, state

officials, departments of health, national guard, American Legion, and others engaged in the common problem. The organization comprises shelter, food supply, medical supply, boat control, railway transportation, accounting, and other necessary working divisions. Due to the fine devotion and spirit of all these organizations, it is possible to say that there is practically none in the territory behind the flood crest who is not now receiving sufficient food, shelter, and medical attention. The states are preserving order and have taken vigorous measures to maintain public health. There is suffering incident to the flood, but it has been minimized in every way humanly possible. [160]

Hoover's attention followed the flood crest as it moved south. He ordered the headquarters to relocate to New Orleans on May 26, where the Red Cross focused on immediate relief for those in the path of the flood crest. Hoover once again made a live radio appeal to the American public. His speech from New Orleans highlighted a special hour-and-a-half-long program, which included an introduction from M.H. Aylesworth in Chicago at 7:00 p.m. and musical performances of southern melodies from New York. [161]

Hoover wanted to focus on rehabilitation in the Mid-South after the flood crest passed, but he faced problems in raising money. The federal government made no immediate appropriations to the affected area; rather, President Coolidge asked the public to donate to the Red Cross. On April 22, he issued a proclamation to the nation stating that the "government is giving such aid as lies within its powers…but the burden of caring for the homeless rests upon the agency designated by Government charter to provide relief in disaster: the American National Red Cross." Congress had adjourned in early spring, so it could do nothing until December unless called into special session by the president, but the aloof Coolidge refused to take that step. Instead, he directed private agencies to pay the cost of direct relief. Coolidge did not even visit the devastated regions, opting on June 6 to take his annual summer vacation in the Black Hills of South Dakota, far from the Mississippi Valley. Coolidge appointed a flood commission, issued calls for relief funds, steadfastly refused to summon a special session of Congress and argued that the emergency would be over before Congress could act. [162]

Hoover realized the Red Cross could not completely finance rescue and relief operations. He left New Orleans for Baton Rouge on the evening of April 29 and continued to Memphis and then Washington for the Pan-American economic crisis. While in the capital, he and Jadwin met with the president on May 2 and convinced Coolidge to double the request for donations for the relief fund, raising the minimum quota to $10 million. Hoover also suggested that the federal government work with banks to provide farmers and merchants with immediate loans to help them rebuild.[163]

Coolidge stubbornly refused to release federal funds for relief, despite the pleas from Hoover and leaders in the flooded areas. He ignored a request for financial aid made by H.L. Remmer on behalf of a committee composed of the University of Arkansas Extension Department, the Missouri Pacific Agricultural Department, Rock Island Railroad, Cotton Belt Railroad and various seed and implement companies. Senators Robert LaFollette (R) of Wisconsin and Royal Copeland (D) of New York added their voices to the chorus of those asking the president to call a special session of Congress. Copeland stated in a telegram to Coolidge that funds from private sources would not completely finance care of the refugees and that flood victims "are entitled to look to Congress for assistance." LaFollette said that Coolidge's reluctance to deal with the crisis appeared "political in character." He pointed out that Congress passed seventy acts appropriating $20 million between 1803 and 1916 for flood victims around the world. Since 1916, Congress had raised $9 million for aid for the United States and countries abroad. LaFollette said, "This flood is the greatest disaster in our history affecting a large number of citizens, caused by the floods of navigable streams over which the federal government has jurisdiction and for which must assume responsibility. It is plainly the duty of the president to call Congress in an extra session at once."[164]

Groups meeting in Memphis also voiced the need for federal aid. The National Drainage Association, representing over seventy-five drainage districts, established a headquarters in Memphis on May 25 and met at the Gayoso Hotel, where it drafted a request for funds to repair canals, levees and ditches. The Interstate Seed Crushers Association met the same day at the Chisca Hotel. The group lauded the work of Hoover and drafted a resolution requesting that Coolidge call a special session of Congress to address the need for immediate funds for relief and long-term flood control.[165]

Hoover announced his reconstruction plans on May 28, despite the fact that the Red Cross failed to raise adequate funds and Congress had not met in a special session to consider more relief legislation. Instead, Hoover encouraged state reconstruction corporations to lend money to farmers, sell these loans to the Federal Intermediate Credit Corporation and use the proceeds to make more loans. He strongly encouraged banks in affected areas and the captains of industries of the day to provide working capital for the banks by buying stock in them.[166]

Hoover hoped that business leaders would respond with the same enthusiasm as Memphians had for calls for money, donations and volunteerism. Hoover ordered the establishment of credit organizations in Mississippi, Arkansas and Louisiana to make short-term loans to farmers. Leading bankers and businessmen, aided by counterparts in the North, set up temporary credit corporations. However, wealthy southerners showed little enthusiasm for the program, forcing Hoover to take more direct actions.[167]

The writer of an editorial in the *Jackson Daily News* complained, "Incidentally, the city of Memphis, which draws more business from the Mississippi Delta than it does from the state of Tennessee, has not subscribed a penny to the capital stock. The banks and clearing house of that city were invited to send representatives to the Jackson meeting and ignored the invitation. Memphis has profited rather than lost by the flood disaster, purchases by the Red Cross from merchants of that city for relief work amounting to hundreds of thousands of dollars."

R.E. Kennington, head of the Mississippi Rehabilitation Corporation, defended Memphis by pointing out that Mississippi businesses, other than lumber, oil and public utilities, had offered little as well. He said that Memphis bankers and businessmen still waited for a representative of the Mississippi Rehabilitation Corporation to come to them to clarify details of the organization before raising the requested $100,000. L.O. Crosby, Mississippi director of flood relief and rehabilitation, also complained about the slow response to subscriptions to the rehabilitation finance corporation from Mississippians. He broadcast a second appeal on May 20, hoping for greater participation as rehabilitation committees prepared to close Red Cross camps.[168]

Several days later, Memphians still had not made progress, so Hoover returned to Memphis determined to get the city's financial leaders to cooperate. He met with the following Memphis Chamber of Commerce members: Robert Brinkley Snowden, S.E. Ragland, J.D. McDowell, Frank Hayden, J.P. Norfleet, W.R. King, C. Arthur Bruce, J.M. Johnson, L.O. Crosby, Eldridge Armistead, R.O. Johnson, J.A. Riechman, O.F. Soderstrom and L.M. Statton. Hoover did not have time to waste and had little patience for the Memphians. The group formed a large circle extending to the right and left of Hoover in a spacious corner room of an uptown hotel. Hoover told them to raise money by the end of the day or he would resettle African American sharecroppers in the North. The bankers, many of whom owned plantations in Arkansas, feared that if they failed to comply Hoover would follow through with his threat. The organization agreed to raise $200,000, leaving the details to member C. Arthur Bruce.[169]

Thirty minutes later, Hoover emerged from the meeting smiling to reporters and said, "It was a fine spirit. The intent was there from the start. There was but little discussion except as to the method to be used in apportioning the fund. That part of it was just pure, simple, and sensible business." Hoover outlined a plan he wanted the Memphis Rehabilitation Committee to follow to raise money for use in Arkansas and Mississippi. Half the money would go to the Mississippi Rehabilitation Corporation, based in Jackson and organized with a capital stock of $1 million. Hoover promised that "Northern capital" would match every dollar raised. Hoover intended for the Red Cross to move farmers and tenants back to their lands and provide houses or tents, stock, seed, farm implements and food until June 9. The Mississippi Rehabilitation Corporation would then make reasonable loans secured by crop mortgages until January 1, 1928. Stockholders would then share the profits or losses pro rata following an orderly liquidation. Hoover concluded the interview and left for Little Rock that evening before returning to the levee break at McCrae, Louisiana, the following day.[170]

The chamber of commerce members proceeded with Hoover's wishes in earnest. Bankers raised $50,000 the day after the meeting with Hoover and promised to raise the rest within a few days. The Federal Intermediate Credit Bank promised to match funds with $4 to every $1 raised by the Mississippi Rehabilitation Corporation. A chamber representative stated, "The present campaign is not for charity, but [it] is the soundest business investment. The industrial, mercantile, and banking interests of Memphis are intimately involved with those of Arkansas and Mississippi." The organization elected R. Brinkley Snowden as permanent chairman and put other members in charge of the various divisions assigned to raise certain quotas: Frank Hayden, finance chairman, $50,000; J.C. Lutz, cotton chairman, $20,000; C. Arthur Bruce, lumber chairman, $25,000; Hays Flowers, retail and hotels chairman, $35,000; L.M. Stratton, wholesale manufacturers chairman, $50,000; and T.H. Tutwiler, utilities, newspapers, builders and transportation chairman, $20,000.[171]

The Memphis division alone raised $40,000 of its $50,000 quota in two hours on Saturday, May 28. Chairmen reported impressive gains during their meeting at the chamber of commerce on May 30. The wholesale division raised $10,500, with subscriptions of $5,000 from Plough Chemical Company and $2,000 from the Reichman-Crosby Company. The utilities division received half of its quota with money raised from newspapers and automobile businesses. The committee met again on May 31 to review progress and outline a plan to quickly conclude the campaign. Members took to the field to recruit contributors in order to reach their quota by the next week.[172]

Hoover pushed local businessmen to make the necessary subscriptions and tried to make them appear as worthwhile investments. Chairman Snowden said:

> In subscribing to this fund, Memphis is given the opportunity to aid our friends and neighbors in Mississippi and Arkansas in a plan under which rehabilitation of the flooded areas can be accomplished, credit can be stabilized, and confidence of the people of the South fully established in the ability and willingness of their own business and financial institutions to take care of their needs. To fail to meet our obligation would mean that the people of the flooded areas in the South would have to turn to the bankers and businessmen of other sections of the country, asking them for help that would come as a donation rather than an investment. The two hundred thousand dollars that Memphis is asked to subscribe is, on the contrary, not a gift, but an investment that will bring certain returns. The money used in rebuilding the flooded areas in Mississippi and Arkansas will put farmers, merchants, and banks on a basis where not only will the ill effects of the flood be overcome, but from which an era of business activity and prosperity will result.[173]

Hoover felt sympathy for the economic status of the flooded areas and favored federal funding for improved levees. President Coolidge, however, did not. The ensuing legislative battle and struggles between the military and civilians would last months while the people in the Mississippi Valley waited anxiously for protection from the Mississippi River. Entertainer Will Rogers joked that the government would put off legislation "with the hope that those needing relief will perhaps have conveniently died in the meantime."[174]

Flood survivors digging through mud and debris in the Mississippi Valley demanded that the federal government do something to keep another disaster like this from happening again. Official reports indicated that 250 people died during the flood and over 160,000 families lost their homes, although actual figures reached much higher numbers. The engineers' levees failed to hold back the river as promised, and Hoover's flood commission responded with labels such as "natural disaster" and "act of God." However, people in the valley would no longer accept the same old excuses. They realized that this flood, as well as the previous floods, resulted largely from man-made problems. They wanted solutions rather than explanations, and they wanted action now.[175]

Chapter 6
GOOD SAMARITAN CITY
OF THE MISSISSIPPI

The world is looking Memphis-ward. The greatest flood of the century is upon us, and these unfortunate men and women...are appealing to Memphis and it's a duty we cannot, must not, dodge.[176]
—*Gene Lewis, manager of the Lyceum Theater, 1927*

On April 19, Mayor Paine received the first contribution to the local Red Cross relief fund—not from Memphians but rather from a naval crew thousands of miles away. The men aboard the Omaha-class light cruiser *Memphis* (CL-13) cabled their donation through the Thomas Cook & Son steamship agency in London, England, once they heard about the disaster in the Mississippi Valley. They had a special fondness for Memphis, not only because their ship bore the city's name but also because the mayor's daughter, Elizabeth "Sugar" Paine, sponsored the ship's christening on April 17, 1924, in Philadelphia.[177]

During the summer of 1925, the ship's commander, Henry Lackey, took the *Memphis* on a goodwill tour with the Pacific Fleet to Australia and New Zealand. The next year, he sailed *Memphis* to the Mediterranean, relieving USS *Pittsburgh* (CA-4) as the flagship of U.S. Naval Forces in Europe, making port calls along the North African littoral and European shores. *Memphis* made port calls in Spain, Greece, Ireland and Germany before completing its European tour of duty by embarking Charles Lindbergh in Southampton, England, on June 3, 1927, and his aircraft, Spirit of St. Louis, at Cherbourg on June 11, 1927, and returning them to the United States.[178]

Light cruiser USS *Memphis* (CL-13). *Courtesy of Library of Congress.*

Upon receipt of the donation, Mayor Paine said, "To my mind this is an expression of the highest ascension of the human spirit that though thousands of miles away these brave American sailors appreciate the distress of Memphis's neighbors and are the first to respond with material relief and aid. I will take pleasure tomorrow in turning over the cable money order for two hundred dollars to W.B. Bayless, chairman of the funds and general relief committee of the local American Red Cross."[179]

Many people did not know the address of the Red Cross headquarters, so they sent their donations directly to the mayor's office. Paine personally handled checks and sent thank-you letters to everyone from the Chattanooga Red Cross and C.M. Kittle of Sears and Roebuck, who donated thousands of dollars, to individuals who donated as little as two dollars. He also recruited knowledgeable volunteers to work with Henry Baker and personally requested additional vessels and crews directly from the secretary of the navy in Vicksburg.[180]

Donations poured in as news spread across the country and around the world about the disaster in the Mississippi Valley. The national Red Cross raised $500,000 of the $5 million requested within three hours of President Coolidge's appeal on April 25. Governor Al Smith appealed

President Coolidge accepts a donation for Red Cross relief from Elizabeth Anne Stitt, daughter of Theodore Stitt, commander in chief of the Veterans of Foreign Wars. *Courtesy of Library of Congress.*

to New Yorkers to donate, and Will Rogers traveled by airplane to New York City for a performance at the new Ziegfeld Theatre to help raise money. New Yorkers contributed over $1 million by May 3; this included $150,000 from John D. Rockefeller and $50,000 from J.P. Morgan. The

French Red Cross donated money and anti-typhoid serum, and the Belgian ambassador Baron De Cartier conveyed the sympathies of King Albert's government to Secretary of State Frank B. Kellogg on April 29 for the Mississippi Valley flood victims. King George of England sent Coolidge a telegram on May 2 expressing his sympathy as well. He wrote, "I have heard with profound sorrow of the serious loss of life and damage to property caused by the floods in the Mississippi Valley and I hasten to offer my heartfelt sympathy both to you and to all those who are suffering from the result of the present disaster."[181]

The Red Cross worked closely with the local newspapers, the *Commercial Appeal* and the *Memphis Evening Appeal*, to raise money and collect material donations for the refugees from local sources. The newspapers even listed donors in order to encourage greater participation in the drive. The *Commercial Appeal* raised thousands of dollars from Memphians from all walks of life— from $2,500 from Columbian Mutual Life Insurance agents to change donated by children. Businesses proudly followed their examples, including the Van Vleet Mansfield Drug Company, which donated over $100 in much-needed medical supplies, and the Memphis Clearing House Association,

Ellis Auditorium. *Courtesy of the Memphis and Shelby County Room, Memphis Public Library and Information Center.*

which gave $7,500. Memphians dropped off clothing donations with city crews in trucks waiting in public parks or gave to Boy Scouts canvassing neighborhoods. Managers of Bry's Department Store and the Memphis Retail Furniture Dealers Association sent trucks to homes of those wishing to donate clothing and other goods, and Tom Estes of the Graham-Merrin Company sent trucks throughout the city to collect food and vegetables for the fairgrounds refugees. By April 22, the Memphis Red Cross had received nearly $10,000, along with overcoats, shoes, bedding and tents gathered at Ellis Auditorium.[182]

Hundreds of theaters around the country held benefits to raise money for the national Red Cross relief fund. Movie stars took the opportunity to make huge donations, including Coleen Moore, who paid $1,000 for her seat at a fundraiser at the Metropolitan Theater in Los Angeles. Representative Sol Bloom of New York asked the forty-four theater managers of New York City to set aside a "flood relief night" to raise money for the Red Cross in the Mississippi Valley. The Lafayette Theater staged a "monster midnight performance" featuring Bill "Bojangles" Robinson, Butterbeans and Susie and Sissle and Blake on May 17 that raised $2,500. A midnight show at Boston's National Theater raised another $1,000, while a program featuring May Alix, Frankie Jaxon and Louis Armstrong's Orchestra on May 6 at Chicago's Apollo Theater raised $200.[183]

Benefits sponsored by local theaters contributed greatly to the drive. Gene Lewis, manager of the Lyceum Theater, organized a show to raise money at the Loew's Theater with the help of C.B. Stiff, manager of Loew's, and A.B. Morrison, manager of the Pantages Theater. Stiff received a copy of the movie *Señorita* starring Bebe Daniels a month early for the occasion. The event opened with Boris Morris and the Palace Concert Orchestra performing "Mr. Jazz in Person," followed by vaudeville acts, including the Pantages dance team, a sketch by the Gene Lewis–Olga Worth Stock Company, ukulele and songs by Foy Witherspoon, a dance review by Mildred Crewe and the Girls, the Seven Aces from the Peabody Hotel, the Marie Lloyd dancers and operatic soprano from Marie Henri Hamilton. Doors opened at 9:30 p.m., and the show began thirty minutes later. Stiff did not charge admission, but the staff collected cash donations from the audience during intermissions.[184]

Manager Eddie J. Sullivan took advantage of relaxed blue laws to organize a seven thirty Sunday night show at the Loew's State Theater to raise money as well. Vaudeville performers, musicians and stagehands donated their time, and the Junior League volunteered as ushers. Sharp's Plectrum Orchestra performed, as well as the Washington Syncopators of the Cortese Brothers' East End Garden. John L. Franconi of the local branch of the Film Booking Offices of America supplied a copy of *Naughty Nanette*, featuring Memphis favorite Viola Dana. Balton and Sons, General Outdoor Advertising and Pilcher Printing supplied posters, and the fire department loaned a truck for advertisement. Their efforts helped draw such a large crowd that the theater called the police department to help maintain order. The first show quickly filled to capacity, while those who could not get in waited for the second show. The following morning, the *Memphis Evening Appeal* staff gave the Red Cross $3,620.00, including an additional $164.16 over the $0.50 cover charge donated by attendees.[185]

Jean Johnson, a leader in musical circles in Memphis, held a meeting with Mrs. R. Brinkley Snowden at her studio at the Gayoso Hotel on April 26 to organize a concert for the following Sunday. They planned the event to begin with an address by Secretary Hoover, which would be followed by a performance by the Loew's Palace Theater Symphony Orchestra. Seats at the auditorium sold for $0.50, except for box seats sold by the Nineteenth Century Club for $1.50. The Memphis Garden Club donated flowers to decorate the stage, and Junior League members again acted as ushers. The Boy Scouts hung posters advertising the event, while the Memphis Street Railway Company conductors carried announcements on their cars. Unfortunately, the busy commerce secretary could not attend. Hoover wrote to promoter Jean Johnson expressing his regrets for having to leave for Washington: "It had been my hope almost to the last minute to appear at this occasion." Johnson offered refunds for those who purchased tickets specifically to hear Hoover, while Mayor Paine introduced Henry Baker, who filled in for Hoover midway through the program.[186]

Tennessee state law prohibited theater owners from showing movies on Sundays; however, they received a special dispensation so that they could show movies during non-church hours in order to raise money for the Red Cross. Even so, Paine kept a careful watch on the theater owners. The mayor wanted to keep the Sunday shows under tight control in order to avoid any possible scandal. He had the Red Cross issue special permits to participating theaters and told them to place their staff in box offices to monitor the bookkeeping. As an additional precaution, Paine went so far as to tell Commissioner Thomas Allen to visit the theaters to keep an eye on the Red Cross staff.[187]

Memphis theater owners took advantage of the flood crisis to give the public a taste of outlawed Sunday entertainment. Normally, theaters could not show movies on Sundays, but many hoped the crisis could help change the law. State senators argued over a bill permitting Shelby County to vote on exemption from the state law prohibiting Sunday motion pictures and theatrical performances. Theater owners had high hopes when the state senate passed the Sunday motion picture referendum on April 22 with a seventeen-to-five vote. The Shelby County delegation anticipated that the bill would pass easily in the House.[188]

Representative McCleish of Haywood County broke the ranks of Memphis supporters when he called on members to support the biblical command to rest on the seventh day by daring them to "vote for the bill and then go home and show their faces in church." Even so, the Sunday movie bill passed fifty-five to twenty through the state House of Representatives on April 25. However, it proved a short-lived victory. Governor Austin Peay had vetoed a similar bill two years earlier and promised to do the same with the new bill since it applied only to Shelby County. The bill failed to override Peay's veto in the Tennessee House of Representatives on April 27.[189]

Sunday benefit shows continued in Memphis despite the failure of the bill. The Pantages Theater manager, A.B. Morrison, presented another Sunday evening flood benefit show featuring vaudeville acts, news reels and the movie *Whispering Wires*, starring Anita Stewart. The DeMolay Chapter sponsored a benefit at the Loew's Palace Theater on May 8. Audiences saw the movies *Ain't Love Funny* and *Now You Tell One* for fifty cents a ticket.[190]

Churches and neighborhood groups held fundraisers as well. The Salon Circle held a card party at the Rex YMCA on the afternoon of April 27, and First Methodist Church, led by Dr. Clovis G. Chappell, collected money during church services. The Little German Band of Loew's State Theater performed in Court Square and marched to the Peabody Hotel, while the North Memphis Civic Improvement Club and the Leroy Pope Parent-Teacher Association sponsored music programs on Sunday, May 1, at 7:00 p.m. and 9:00 p.m. at the Suzore Theater. The programs featured Harry Philwin's Entertainers, Mary Lloyd and her dancers, R. Roy Coates with his saxophone band and Fritz Lawless.[191]

The Memphis Red Cross continued to receive donations locally and from around the country. The *Commercial Appeal* office received over $9,000 on April 26 alone from across the region, bringing the total raised locally for the Red Cross to $35,000. Donations increased after Al Jolson asked every American to send in a dime to the Red Cross during his April 30 national radio broadcast. Amounts from $0.10 to $5,000.00 poured into local Red Cross chapters around the country. Just four days later, George

Morris, editor of the *Evening Appeal*, handed Henry Baker a check for $79,571.00 for donations received by the newspaper, bringing the total raised in Memphis to almost $100,000.00.[192]

Local organizations and businesses also made significant contributions: the American Telephone and Telegraph Company donated $25,000; the local Knights of Columbus donated $1,000 on May 7; Piggly Wiggly donated $1,000 on May 9; and the Ames Plantation in Grand Junction, Tennessee, donated $525. Contributions began to lag by the end of May, but the Red Cross drive still managed to raise $123,401 by May 26.[193]

The flooded area through the valley covered fifteen thousand square miles, an area larger than Belgium, three times the size of Connecticut and almost as large as Switzerland. The Red Cross realized that it faced not only an immense relief problem but also a potentially staggering health crisis resulting from river water polluting local water and food supplies. The agency provided provisions, clothing, shelter and medical care for over 600,000 refugees. The Red Cross established temporary hospitals to augment overcrowded local medical facilities and refugee camps. It sheltered the homeless and closely supervised and regulated life in the congested facilities in order to prevent outbreaks of smallpox, typhoid fever and other communicable diseases.[194]

The Red Cross national medical director, Dr. William R. Redden, understood the dangers presented by the Mississippi Valley flood and knew how to combat the health threats. Redden's previous experience with malaria included directing relief work in Macedonia in 1924, where he used fifteen tons of quinine to save the population from the disease. Redden saw the potential for a similar situation in the Mississippi Valley because of the lack of clean drinking water. He expected the many refugees who resorted to drinking river water to contract typhoid within the next two weeks, so he began smallpox and typhoid inoculations immediately. He used 150,000 pounds of chlorate of lime and a railroad car load of oil per county in addition to other disinfectants to combat disease. Dr. French of Memphis traveled to Hughes with vaccines, while Redden sent another supply of vaccines to Blytheville. Two African American physicians from Memphis, Dr. R.S. Field and Dr. Thornton, traveled to Greenville to care for African American refugees.[195]

Redden realized that state and local authorities lacked preparation and funding to handle the health crisis, so he called a conference in Memphis on April 28 to organize treatment efforts. He invited health officers from the seven states affected by the flood, the U.S. Army Fourth and Seventh Corps, the U.S. Navy, the U.S. Public Health Service and Henry Baker to meet and coordinate the program. After hearing reports of isolated outbreaks of smallpox, measles, mumps, typhoid, malaria, tuberculosis and influenza, the group focused its immediate efforts on Arkansas and Mississippi—which it determined faced the gravest health problems of the flooded states—and decided to use the Red Cross medical service as a clearing house to furnish supplies and personnel to local health units.[196]

With the assistance of Dr. John McMullen; Dr. Allen McLaughlin, superintendent of the U.S. Marine Hospital at St. Louis; and Dr. L.L. Lumsden, a pioneer in rural sanitation, Redden's program proved a great success. The immunization program helped prevent further outbreaks of typhoid and smallpox by providing over eighty thousand people with vaccinations by May 5. Redden also isolated the sick in order to contain outbreaks; however, he still faced the issues of unsanitary conditions left by receding floodwaters and the lack of suitable drinking water and milk.[197]

Surgeon General Hugh S. Cummins suggested a conference of state health officials to plan a program to handle the Mississippi Valley's "sanitation problem of great magnitude." Cummins led a conference in Washington, D.C., on May 21 to coordinate federal and state health agencies and the Red Cross in disease control in the flooded areas. Agencies provided workers and supplies and agreed to meet again in Memphis to plan their further actions.[198]

The U.S. Public Health Service transferred its field management to Memphis, with Dr. John McMullen acting as liaison with state boards of health and making sure they had adequate supplies of smallpox and typhoid vaccines. Experts from Baltimore arrived in Memphis to assist McMullen on May 24: Maryland state health officers Dr. W.C. Stone, Dr. R.G. Beachley and Dr. B.H. DeSomoskeoy; epidemiologist Dr. V. L. Elliott; Dr. James A. Doull, associate professor at Hopkins School of Hygiene; and Dr. Collinson. McMullen assigned each to take charge of a district. Directors of the Red Cross Nursing Service, Elizabeth Fox, Malinde Harvey and Clara D. Noyes, mobilized and supervised nurses in the refugee camps. In all, doctors and health workers from twenty-two states volunteered, including 329 nurses and one overly enthusiastic sanitary volunteer who arrived armed with a shotgun to enforce camp hygiene.[199]

McMullen realized that malaria continued to present a serious threat as the floodwaters receded. He contacted Surgeon General Cummins and asked for permission to invite mosquito and malaria expert Dr. Joseph Augustin LePrince to join the team. Cummins promptly approved the request and wired McMullen the authority. LePrince reported to the Red Cross headquarters in Memphis on May 21 and met with McMullen and Redden that morning to discuss his plans for malaria control before leaving for Arkansas to begin his work. He had over twenty-two thousand screen doors and over twenty-five thousand screen windows made and installed to protect people from disease-carrying mosquitoes. He initially intended to screen just the homes of malaria carriers but expanded the program to include other homes as a way to promote the use of screens.[200]

The U.S. Public Health Service also made advances in combating pellagra (a disease resulting from a diet deficient in niacin marked by dermatitis, gastrointestinal disorders and mental disturbances). Dr. Joseph Goldberger found an unusually high number of cases due to economic conditions resulting from poor cotton yields over the previous five years. Goldberger directed the Red Cross to distribute a pure culture of brewer's yeast in powdered form as a dietary supplement—the first operation on such a scale. They gave over five tons to refugees in flooded areas between August 15 and October 18 and continued to distribute the supplement into the following year.[201]

State health departments reported that the flooded areas had a much lower rate of typhoid fever, infant diarrhea, smallpox, malaria and other communicable diseases than in the previous five years due to the program's success. Hoover called Redden's efforts a "triumph for public health and scientific medicine." The U.S. Public Health Service continued operation of the health units with additional funding from the Rockefeller Foundation. The two organizations had worked together previously in 1916 to eradicate malaria-carrying mosquitoes in Crossett County, Arkansas, but they could not expand the program because of the shortage of funds resulting from the agricultural recession of the 1920s. The success of Redden's program gave them the opportunity to continue programs to make long-lasting improvements to the health of Southerners.[202]

The Shelby County Health Department took steps to protect local residents from possible epidemics. Dr. L.M. Graves had free clinics opened at Shelby County schools to inoculate students against typhoid, while director of child hygiene Dr. C.W. Polk gave shots and a physician from the Shelby County Anti-Tuberculosis Society made chest examinations. They began with the George J. James School in Bartlett and the Eads Colored School on April 27 and continued through the beginning of June visiting Normal, Capleville, White Station, Arlington, Messick, Treadwell, Kerrville, Millington Colored School, Millington Central High, Lucy and the Shelby

County Training School. Dr. Polk held night clinics to inoculate working people against typhoid in flooded areas in North Memphis. He gave shots at Hollywood School on May 2 and 3 and Manassas Colored School on May 4, 5 and 6. The Illinois Central Railroad officials ordered vaccinations of its approximately fifteen thousand employees against typhoid, with the local company surgeon, Dr. J.A. Vallery, supervising the vaccinations of the nearly four thousand employees in Memphis. Dr. Graves and Dr. Polk continued giving typhoid inoculations to anyone over three years of age at Messick and Treadwell Schools through the beginning of June. They offered shots at Kerrville School, Millington High School and Millington Colored School on May 30 and Lucy School and the Shelby County Colored Training School on June 2.[203]

Wolf River, just north of the city, and Nonconnah Creek, to the south, began to back up as the level of the Mississippi River rose to record heights. In addition, smaller bayous throughout the city that drained into these tributaries overflowed into nearby neighborhoods and even downtown areas. By mid-April, water from the overflowing Lick Creek covered parts of North Memphis around Vollintine Street and Tutwiler Street between

Flooding around St. Joseph's Hospital. *Author's collection.*

Memphis and the Mississippi Valley Flood of 1927

Mules pull a wagon through chest-deep water along Jackson Avenue. *Author's collection.*

A wall of sandbags protects a railyard in Memphis, May 5, 1927. *Courtesy of the University of Mississippi Archives and Special Collections.*

Idlewild and McLean. Areas around St. Joseph's Hospital also flooded, even though the pumps at the mouth of Bayou Gayoso ran at nearly full capacity, pouring 1,300 cubic feet of water per second over the upper levee into the Wolf River. A reporter boasted that manufacturers, lumbermen and railroad interests felt that "Memphis was never better prepared to withstand high water and can successfully fend off stages of forty-eight to forty-nine feet in the low-lying industrial districts to the north and south." Despite his assurances, Memphians, who after seeing debris, dead livestock and even houses floating down the river for weeks, became increasingly anxious when they saw floodwater at their doorsteps.[204]

Backwater from North Memphis bayous flooded three hundred homes in the Hollywood neighborhood, forcing evacuations for the first time since the flood of 1913. As the water continued to rise, a city engineer told reporters, "Absolutely nothing can be done to relieve the situation. We can only wait for the Mississippi River to go down." Residents of this largely African American neighborhood stacked belongings on homemade skiffs and waded through

Residents of north Memphis move household goods out of homes on a makeshift skiff. *Author's collection.*

View of north Memphis neighborhood after a backwater spillover from a nearby bayou. *Author's collection.*

the water to higher ground. The Wolf River washed over the North Second Street Bridge, and early morning rains on April 20 halted streetcars on the Hollywood line at Chelsea and Breedlove. Water rose so high that city workers had to help people from their homes. On one occasion, a Spencer-Sturla ambulance crew had to rescue bedridden Mae McLaughlin from her home on North Second Street after floodwaters rose to four feet.[205]

Commissioner Luther F. Jones made an inspection of eastern Shelby County and discovered thousands of dollars of damage to roads after the river stage reached 43.5 feet and 3.8 inches of rainfall caused water to rise in already flooded areas in the city and county. Workers cleared driftwood at the Big Creek Bridge on Millington Road that threatened to dam up the river and damage the bridge, and Highway 1 closed while crews made repairs after a washout following a break in the Beaver Levee. Water covered Hindman Ferry Road, Rugby Park Road, the Jones Avenue neighborhood and Paine Avenue near the Wolf River Sand Company. The overflowing Big Creek flooded Mount Vernon and Woodstock Road, and the Loosahatchie washed out Benjestown Road. The extensive flooding finally forced Commissioners Hale and Jones to close all highways in northern Shelby County, as well as O.K. Robertson and Raleigh-Millington Roads.[206]

The South Memphis pumping station had only a limited effect on bringing the water levels down around Nonconnah Creek. Heavy rain

Flooded homes near Memphis. *Author's collection.*

Two-story house near Memphis covered almost to the roof by floodwaters. *Author's collection.*

caused the tributary to spill over its banks, creating problems with roadways into Mississippi. Traffic became congested as drivers had to slow down to maneuver around the "hump" of sandbags that held back floodwaters from the point where Horn Lake Road intersected with the levee. Floodwaters washed out a small bridge across Horn Lake Road and caused the closing of the Florida Midwest Highway, one of the principal routes into Mississippi.[207]

Memphis and the Mississippi Valley Flood of 1927

Floodwaters from Nonconnah Creek approaching railyards. *Courtesy of The University of Mississippi Archives and Special Collections.*

The flood crest reached Memphis on April 23 with a record-breaking stage of 45.8 feet, surpassing the record set fourteen years earlier and pushing the city's flood control measures to their limits. Workers faced a difficult struggle to save the levees as time and resources ran short. With manpower in short supply, city officials conscripted prisoners from the county workhouse to help out. The shortage of materials and muddy roads slowed work, but to make matters worse thousands of snakes—including poisonous water moccasins—took refuge from the water in the undergrowth along the levee, rendering the work especially dangerous.[208]

Chief engineer William Fowler ordered crews to bolster flood protection downtown in anticipation of a record flood stage following the Good Friday storms. He publicly assured Memphians that pumping stations stood ready and that the twelve-block-long levee from Auction to Bickford would hold against any flood stage up to fifty-two feet. However, with water lapping near the top of the navy yard levee, the engineer wanted to take every precaution against a possible crevasse. Workers added a foot and a half of sandbags to the levee along the riverfront protecting the Jones and Laughlin Steel Plant at the navy yard and bolstered the protective wall around the Illinois Central Railroad. Crews aided by a steam shovel worked through the night to reinforce the levee, and navy yard workers extended the protective wall from the foot of Jackson Avenue across the railroad tracks and raised the main levee in anticipation of the rising water.[209]

Levee at Memphis. *Courtesy of the University of Mississippi Archives and Special Collections.*

Debris along levee at Memphis. *Courtesy of the University of Mississippi Archives and Special Collections.*

Memphis and the Mississippi Valley Flood of 1927

View from the customhouse of the mouth of the overflowing Wolf River and partially submerged Mud Island. *Courtesy of the Memphis and Shelby County Room, Memphis Public Library and Information Center.*

Flooding from backwater interrupted traffic and caused damage throughout the city and county. It took two weeks before police could reopen flooded roads in Shelby County. Weaver Road and Delta Highway/Lakeview Road opened in May, and crews removed sandbags that held back water from Horn Lake Road. However, Memphis still felt the effects of the flood for weeks as streets flooded periodically from overflowing bayous and neighborhoods lost telephone service.[210]

Continuing rain in the last weeks of April caused havoc downtown and on the riverfront. Firemen and police spent hours rescuing stranded motorists and homeowners who woke to find water in their houses, and a cave-in at the foot of Illinois Street buried two small vacant houses and slowed traffic. As storms continued, lightning struck one of the pinnacles of St. Mary's Cathedral, tearing a hole in the roof, and water damaged the ten-thousand-dollar organ.[211]

City and railroad officials had concerns over possible long-term damage resulting from the rain and high water. Slides worsened after the river current shifted in 1912, and a 1924 cave-in caused a work train to fall into the river. Many had worries that the current flood would cause similar problems along the waterfront. On May 27, local, federal and railroad officials met to discuss the results of a study of the weakening riverbanks and plan a course of action to repair them. Those present at the meeting included Mayor Paine;

city engineer Will Fowler; Major Donald Connolly of the U.S. Army Corps of Engineers; Colonel F.G. Jonah of the Frisco Railroad; K.G. Williams, chief engineer of Union Railroad; and A.F. Baless, chief engineer of the Illinois Central System in Chicago.[212]

The business community wanted to maintain a positive image for Memphis in order to attract new businesses. Chairman Milton S. Binswanger stated that "the industrial development of the city is a matter of vital importance to every businessman in the community" in a meeting of the Memphis Chamber of Commerce on April 20. Division director A.P. Fant listed inquiries he received for information about the city from businesses interested in relocating there, and the chairman encouraged members to submit suggestions of what industries to approach about coming to Memphis. Binswanger stated, "Memphis has every requisite necessary to industrial progress and with the concerted effort of her businessmen centered on industrial development, unprecedented growth may be confidently expected."[213]

The staff of a Washington newspaper caused a great deal of resentment when it printed a picture of a flooded suburb in Little Rock and mistakenly identified it as Memphis. James Davant, commissioner of the Memphis Freight Bureau, responded in an address on WMC in which he said that Memphis, the "logical distribution point for the South and Southwest," had the advantage of "sitting high and dry on bluffs that protect the city from the greatest overflow in the history of the Mississippi River." Davant also addressed the story of Memphis flooding: "Memphis is not concerned about reports which picture her as being a victim to this flood." He described Memphis as a safe haven immune from the effects of the flood, quoting a press release from the Memphis Chamber of Commerce:

> So far above the water's edge that she does not even need galoshes to keep her feet dry—with her head cool, her heart warm, and her arms outstretched in welcome to thousands of refugees seeking shelter and aid. Memphis stands high above the waters of the Mississippi River swirling by in the worst flood in the history of that mighty stream. In the midst of the flooded area, yet untouched by the flood, safe on her high bluffs, fifty feet above the rushing waters, Memphis is again proving her claim to the title Good Samaritan city of the Mississippi.[214]

However, the idea persisted that Memphis had suffered from widespread flooding. On May 21, Mayor Paine wrote to Ralph Amerman, president of Kiwanis International, to assure him that his organization could carry on with its plans to hold a convention in Memphis. Paine emphasized that the city sits safely above the flooded areas, that the refugees had returned to their homes and that train service operated on a normal schedule. He wrote, "I very much hope that you will fully understand the real facts and let no false rumors of statements lead you to the belief that there is any possibility of danger in coming to Memphis, either because of the flood or because of health conditions."[215]

As the flood crest moved south, Louisiana governor James Thomson, Hoover and Jadwin authorized a plan to divert the flood into the St. Bernard and Plaquemines Parish marshlands in order to save low-lying New Orleans. On April 29, engineers made an unsuccessful attempt to blow a hole in the levee with thirty-nine tons of dynamite across the river at a place called Caernarvon, thirteen miles below Canal Street. They tried again two days later, opening the levee and sending 250,000 cubic feet of water per second through a fur-rich, tall-grass marshland. New Orleans escaped serious damage, but the diversion destroyed much of the marsh traditionally trapped by the Canary Islanders (Isleños), whose eighteenth-century ancestors colonized Louisiana for Spain. The governor of Louisiana, the mayor of New Orleans and other men of industry in the city promised reparations. However, once the flood passed, they soon forgot their promises, and in the end the residents received very little, if any, compensation.[216]

The Red Cross staff moved their headquarters to a larger facility at the Ford plant on Union Avenue one night during the last week of April. The staff completed the move in only an hour, without interrupting the call center's contact with operations in Tennessee, Arkansas, Missouri, Mississippi, Louisiana, Kentucky and Illinois. Major General Mallin Craig of the Fourth Corps in Atlanta arrived on May 1 and remarked that he had never seen so many government agencies work so efficiently with "such absolute lack of friction."[217]

The staff of the Red Cross headquarters in Memphis continued to direct recovery efforts in the camps and rural areas devastated by floodwaters. Mary Barrow Giesen, head of the Agricultural Extension Service in Mississippi, and her counterpart in Arkansas, Connie J. Bonslagle, met in Memphis with W.C. Warburton, director of extension work in the southeastern states, to plan recovery efforts. Giesen directed the activities of Mississippi A&M College and the United States Department of Agriculture in providing instruction to women in the refugee camps about gardening and canning fruits and vegetables. C.P. Doe, a former supply officer in Germany during the post–World War I Allen Relief Expedition, took charge of supply distribution. Bonslagle worked tirelessly to educate rural Arkansans about health issues and recovery efforts. Assistant city manager of Miami, Florida Paul C. Wilcox and prominent Miami citizen E.B. Douglas volunteered with the Red Cross as an expression of appreciation for the help provided to their city by Memphians following the hurricane the previous September. Baker assigned Wilcox to oversee county units in Mississippi, while Douglas acted as Baker's liaison.[218]

The Red Cross relocated its headquarters to New Orleans since the majority of its activities now centered on Louisiana. Baker and his thirty-nine-member staff boarded a special Illinois Central train and left Memphis at 9:30 p.m. on May 25. They took only files, maps and small equipment, leaving behind furniture, file cabinets and typewriters. Many left at the last possible moment with only enough time to gather personal baggage and meet the train. They arrived at seven thirty the following morning and opened the new headquarters an hour later. Fieser, as he left for New Orleans, expressed regret at leaving and conveyed the gratitude of the Red Cross for the entire Memphis staff and the cooperation of everyone in the city.[219]

Baker introduced Earl Kilpatrick as his rehabilitation specialist for the Mid-South on May 18 during a Cooperative Club luncheon. Once the headquarters relocated to New Orleans, he left Kilpatrick in charge of operations in Memphis and assigned A.L. Shaffer to direct relief work in Illinois, Missouri, Tennessee, Kentucky and Arkansas from the Vicksburg office. Kilpatrick began by having staff issue departing refugees with rations for two weeks, as well as tents for those without homes. He distributed farm implements only as necessary and informed planters that he expected them to step up and care for tenants rather than relying on only Red Cross rehabilitation funds.[220]

More severe weather in early May only made the situation worse for the Mid-South. Thunderstorms on May 6 caused flooding around Forrest City, blew away refugees' tents and destroyed buildings, while lightning killed at least 2 people. The storm generated a tornado that struck Clayton, Mississippi. This was followed by more tornadoes three days later that swept through Missouri, Arkansas, Kansas and Texas. A massive tornado swept across eastern Arkansas from northern Louisiana to southeastern Missouri killing over 200 people. The tornado crossed into Missouri and hit Poplar Bluff at 3:15 p.m., striking the business district of the town, killing 60 people, injuring over 150 and leaving only four of the town's thirty-five buildings intact. The Red Cross immediately reassigned Dr.

Redden to oversee the care of victims and issued additional requests for donations from the public.[221]

Mid-Southerners had the additional discomfort of having to endure an earthquake and a series of aftershocks beginning about 2:30 a.m. on May 7. The quakes woke people in a 250-mile radius throughout southern Illinois, southeastern Missouri, eastern Arkansas, western Kentucky, western Tennessee and northern Mississippi. Little damage occurred, but the quakes added to the misery and anxiety of those having to cope with flooding, bad weather and recent tornadoes. Some began to wonder about a connection between the events and worried about more quakes. Brother Joseph of Christian Brothers College, a local earthquake expert, tried to calm nerves by assuring the public that the series of quakes had no connection to the flood. However, others saw the quake as something more ominous. An African American preacher who made it to Memphis after he escaped a Yazoo County refugee camp recounted what he said after being asked to speak to his people for the landowners: "I told my people, and others, too, the Lord sent his flood to baptize sinners, master and servant alike. They were slow in accepting salvation, so He shook the earth, giving a warning to take the first train to Memphis and then to the Promised Land, north or east. I had to leave, so here I am, on my way."[222]

A story circulated in *Time* magazine about a panic-stricken Shetland pony falling into the flooding White River near Forsyth, Missouri. His pasture mate, a mule, turned back from the safety of high ground, dove in the water and dragged the pony ashore by the mane. However, most animals in the flood's path did not fare as well. Farmers often had little or no time to gather their livestock before floodwater swept across their land. Dead animals littered the streets of Greenville following the levee break at Scott's Landing. Workers discovered fourteen dead mules lodged against the wall of the Queen City brick plant. Dead animals littered waterways, farms, urban areas and even trees, raising concerns about disease.[223]

Farmers try to save cattle in a flooded field. *Courtesy of the University of Mississippi Archives and Special Collections.*

Dog stranded on a roof near Murphy, Mississippi. *Courtesy of Library of Congress.*

The Red Cross made efforts to save livestock whenever possible. Farmers donated feed to the Memphis headquarters that river pilots included in their emergency supply shipments to refugee camps. Red Cross workers and refugees from the fairgrounds worked day and night at the end of April, loading as much as one hundred tons of hay at a time aboard steamers bound for Arkansas and Mississippi.[224]

The Izaak Walton League, an environmental organization, provided food and care for wildlife in the flooded areas. Animals survived by taking refuge on any available high ground such as hills and levees and faced many of the same problems as the refugees, including exposure and lack of food. Refugees often shared what little food they had with these pitiful creatures that took refuge with them on levees and hilltops. The Memphis and Forrest City chapters of the league worked together to provide feed to hungry animals beginning in May and contributed boats and crews to rescue and relief efforts. Newspaper stories about their work drew the attention from people around the country who offered to send money and supplies.[225]

Memphis and the Mississippi Valley Flood of 1927

Levees also became a refuge to snakes, which were flooded out of their swampy homes. The *Wabash* left Memphis on April 25 to rescue five hundred flood victims marooned on a levee near Wayside, Mississippi, twelve miles south of Greenville. The refugees had to brave the elements, as well as share the levee with hundreds of snakes. Three died from exposure, and another man suffered a bite from a snake he found in his boot.[226]

The flooding also had an impact on the Mid-South's hardwood industry. On April 25, the Hardwood Manufacturers' Association of Memphis expected 124 lumber mills to shut down because of the flood. However, the devastation exceeded its expectations. By the end of the month, the flood stopped production at over 300 southern mills by either destroying or inundating facilities. Those that survived remained isolated because of washed-out roads. Waterlogged stock had little value in most markets, and workers could use only wet lumber for making cheap cardboard boxes. On the other hand, the *Milwaukee Journal* reported that northern lumber mills profited from the disaster in the South. The disruption in the southern hardwood industry brought about increased prices, enabling northern mills to sell at a profit for the first time in four years.[227]

Economists argued over what effect the flood would have on cotton production. Some thought that the loss of domestic animals, tools and cottonseed would have an impact on the crop, while others felt that the flood would affect only a third of the farms. However, those close to the region had a better feel for the situation. An expert at the Memphis Cotton Exchange believed that farmers might make half a crop if the waters receded in three weeks. He added, "If it does not, God alone knows what will happen."[228]

The economics of cotton cultivation could hardly get worse. It had suffered for years because of overproduction, a reduction of markets and greater competition among domestic growers. United States agriculture expanded during World War I to sell food to Europe, but afterward these countries imported less as they restored their own farms. Despite successive attempts in Congress to provide relief, the agricultural economy of the 1920s experienced an ongoing depression due to overproduction. Falling prices followed at a time when American farmers suffered from heavy debt, driving down wages. The U.S. government's policies only made the situation worse. The Fordney-McCumber Tariff made foreign exports to the United States very expensive, causing Europeans to earn less and therefore spend less on American products. The resulting agricultural depression hit the southern cotton growers hard, especially with increasing competition from the western states.

Overproduction continued even though the U.S. Agriculture Department estimated that floodwaters covered approximately 150,000 bales of cotton in compresses worth about $1,350,000 in the Mississippi Valley. Insurance covered a major portion of the losses, and that may have helped growers desperate to sell their stock. Dr. E.R. Lloyd, secretary of the farm service of the Memphis Chamber of Commerce, and Dr. J.A. Evans of the U.S. Department of Agriculture informed the Agricultural Club of Memphis that the market faced continued cotton overproduction despite the losses due to the flood. Lloyd informed the members at the luncheon at the Hotel Gayoso on May 24 that southern farmers should concentrate on planting other crops, especially corn, wherever possible as they rebuilt their farms.[229]

The battle between federal Prohibition agents and bootleggers continued despite the hazards of operating on high water. Bootleggers, forced out of their usual haunts by floodwaters, built stills in treetops and peddled their wares by boat. The persistent outlaws refused to let the river or the government get in their way. Bootleggers blew up Revenue Speedboat V-10047 at Kennedy Dry Dock at the foot of Beale Street on April 18. Undeterred, agents A.D. Ramsey and Johnson Walker captured a 1,000-gallon still the next day near Crawfordsville. The still contained 10,000 gallons of mash and 100 gallons of liquor, though the lone operator escaped. Officials in May seized twelve giant stills, two with capacities of 750 gallons, and destroyed forty-five vats, each holding 1,000 gallons of mash.[230]

Meanwhile, another wave of water hit the Mississippi Valley beginning at the end of May. By June 15, the river at Memphis crested at thirty-nine feet and remained above flood stage for sixteen days. The Lower Mississippi Valley typically experienced seasonal flooding known as "June rises," but they rarely caused extensive property damage. However, the damaged levees left farmers unprotected. Jadwin met with C.L. Potter, chairman of the Mississippi River Commission, to make plans to repair the broken levees before the rise. Connolly also promised to send his engineers to repair the levee breaks at Dorena, Knowlton's Landing, Laconia Circle and Whitehall before the expected floods. The engineers planned to complete repairs so that farmers could safely plant new crops; however, they failed to deliver on their promise, and the new flood ruined the emerging crops.[231]

Colonel Spalding used the flood to make a case for increased military spending. During his weekly meeting at the Engineers' Club of Memphis he stated, "Military preparedness, decried by pacifists, has been responsible for the rescue work during the Mississippi flood." He compared the underfunded engineer to the underfunded soldier. Like the soldier, the

Levee break at Laconia Circle. *Courtesy of Library of Congress.*

engineer receives only part of the money needed to provide an adequate defense, while at the same time he receives criticism for limited results. He believed "military preparedness is never a waste, but [rather] a bulwark of defense against attack and a reservoir for relief for the Red Cross in case of disaster."[232]

An editorial author celebrated the arrival of Hoover, Fieser, Baker and Jadwin on April 25 but also pointed out that their efforts would have little lasting effect unless the federal government did something about long-term flood control. He wrote that the flood gave Hoover the opportunity to "meditate upon the gross neglect of a nation for a section that has borne the brunt of floods year after year since the vast area to the north was cleared for cultivation." The author concluded, "If this flood does not impel Congress to do its duty, people of the lower Mississippi Valley may well conclude that they occupy about the same relationship to their country that is held by Filipinos, and not quite so desirable a place as that of Nicaraguans and Panamanians."[233]

Chapter 7
POLITICS OF NEW FLOOD CONTROL

*Tax relief, farm relief, flood relief, dam relief—none of these have been
settled, but they are getting them in shape for consideration at the next
session of Congress with the hope that those needing relief will perhaps have
conveniently died in the meantime.*
—*Will Rogers*

Flood control became William Hale Thompson's new calling during his
journey to New Orleans. However, the people of the Mississippi Valley
had little patience for the flamboyant northerner. Refugees gladly accepted
Big Bill's assistance during his trip down the Mississippi River but showed
little interest in his speeches or efforts to attract media attention. Thompson
tried in vain to get the attention of levee workers, who had more concern
about damage from the wakes of Thompson's steamers than anything the
man had to say. Glum and pouting, he clutched the manuscript of a wet and
undelivered speech and wisely kept his distance out of fear of possible gunfire.
In New Orleans, where Thompson intended to end his trip with welcome
speeches and reception committees, masses of citizens gathered—not to
greet but to repel the Chicagoans. Thompson and his party, chagrined and
apologetic, gave $7,000 to various relief organizations.[234]

Undeterred, Thompson told a gathering of Louisiana businessmen that
he and New Orleans mayor Arthur J. O'Keefe would organize a conference
to secure federal funding for flood control. Thompson returned home
and enlisted support from Congressman Martin Madden, chair of the
Appropriations Committee, and Congressman Frank R. Reid, chair of the

House Flood Control Committee. Thompson then publically announced that Chicago would host the Mississippi Valley flood control conference on June 2.[235]

Thompson tried to accommodate President Coolidge's schedule in order to get him to attend. He offered to select a date for the conference to coincide with Coolidge's trip through Chicago on his way to his Black Hills vacation. Coolidge refused out of fear of what a popular flood control convention would do to public opinion and his closely guarded budget.[236]

Coolidge wanted nothing to do with the Mississippi Valley or its problems. Instead, he wanted to vacation far away from the disaster and turned responsibilities over to his war secretary, Dwight F. Davis, who met with Hoover to inspect the flooded areas on May 5. Coolidge tried to justify his decision by telling reporters that there was little he could learn that could not be obtained from others if he remained in Washington.[237]

The president also directed Davis to set up an alternate conference to upstage Thompson. The secretary enlisted prominent legislators, particularly members of the presiding committees, to snub the Chicago convention in favor of the Mississippi River tour sponsored by the recently formed Mississippi Valley Flood Control Association, a Memphis-based advocacy group that represented levee boards and landowners in the Mississippi Valley. Two weeks later, Fred D. Beneke, secretary of the association, led the tour with the help of the Illinois Central Railroad for members of the Senate Commerce Committee, chaired by Senator Wesley L. Jones, and Willis G. Sears and William F. Kopf of Frank Reid's House Flood Control Committee. They gathered at the Hotel Statler in St. Louis on May 14 and left by train at midnight for southeast Missouri and Arkansas. The party arrived in Memphis on the evening of May 17 and left the following day for Greenville.[238]

Another group of congressmen gathered in St. Louis on May 29 joined by Major Connolly of the U.S. Army Corps of Engineers in Memphis. The *Congressional Special*, carrying congressmen and senators, arrived in Memphis late on May 31. The train, composed of a Frisco coach, two Pullman cars, a dining car, a club car and a baggage car, first visited the Missouri levee breaks at New Madrid and Dorena. The party then traveled to Arkansas, where it saw flooded areas around Big Lake, Marked Tree, Jonesboro and Clarendon. Senator Pat Harrison met the party in Memphis and traveled with it on its inspection of Mississippi.[239]

The same day, Rowlett Paine left Memphis by automobile for Thompson's conference in Chicago. Initially, Paine had doubts about the conference because of the lack of support from the president. However, in a letter to Luke Lea on June 7, he described his change of heart after hearing Thompson speak and meeting with the influential committee members. He felt that the committee had a workable plan, and he had high hopes for the eventual meeting with Coolidge.[240]

Driving his automobile through west Tennessee allowed Paine to see the receding floodwaters firsthand, preparing him for his duties as a committee vice-chairman. He arrived at the Hotel Sherman, where people with placards and fife and drum corps met the delegates as they passed through the lobby on their way to the grand ballroom. A band of Chicago high school students, on special vacation for the day, played Thompson's campaign anthem "America First, Last and Always" while a sextet of uniformed Chicago policemen sang along. Thompson mounted a platform under a gigantic banner inscribed with "America First" as over 1,800 delegates to the Mississippi Flood Control Conference clapped their hands and stamped their feet.[241]

Various speakers took the podium to give their views on flood control and the government's handling of the disaster. Among those in attendance were Mayor Arthur O'Keefe of New Orleans; Mayor Victor J. Miller of St. Louis; Senators Smith Brookhart, Pat Harrison and Henrik Shipstead; Edwin Jadwin; Dwight Davis; and Speaker of the House Nicholas Longworth. Paine took the opportunity to praise Hoover's efforts, while other speakers criticized the lack of adequate flood control and called for immediate federal action. Thompson called the flood "an indictment of and challenge to the federal government" and something that "might have been expected in China but not in the rich America with its boasted good government." Senator Henrik Shipstead of Minnesota said, "We have stood around long enough meeting the situation with halfway measures." O'Keefe called upon the federal government to "assume full responsibility" and to "make immediate appropriations."[242]

Coolidge's representatives assured the delegates that the government would soon take action and defended the levee system. Secretary Davis said, "The Mississippi can and must be controlled. The nation whose engineers built the Panama Canal despite seemingly insuperable obstacles can solve the problem of flood control." Major General Jadwin reiterated the need to have levees as the backbone of flood prevention. He believed that even though the current flood covered over twenty thousand miles of land it would have covered up to thirty thousand acres without the levees. He also attacked the popular theory that reforestation would prevent future floods, arguing against the idea that thick forestation slowed the massive flood of 1844.[243]

The three-day conference concluded with a general call for the federal government to take action. The committee passed a resolution introduced by Colonel Bennett H. Clark for the creation of a permanent committee with Mayors O'Keefe, Miller and Paine as vice-chairmen. Senators Longworth and Harrison of Mississippi closed the conference by declaring that Congress should enact temporary legislation for the relief of flood victims. The committee adopted the resolutions calling on the federal government to supply immediate flood relief and requested congressional and presidential action on the prevention of further floods. The delegates intended to draft resolutions recommending methods of flood prevention, but the committee, so divided between adherents of levees, reservoirs, reforesting, spillways and various combinations of these methods, could not agree on a proposal method.[244]

Paine made the motion that Thompson should deliver the resolutions to Coolidge in person, and Roy West, secretary of the Republican National Committee and executive committee member, arranged the meeting. Thompson finally met with Coolidge in early November, and the following summer, Big Bill went on a speaking tour of the Great Plains to generate support of new flood control legislation. He told a St. Paul audience that flood control was nothing less than the "gospel of America." As Coolidge feared, the resulting new permanent executive committee increased the already mounting pressure on Congress for new comprehensive flood control legislation.[245]

Frank Reid, chair of the House Flood Control Committee, inspected the flood-damaged Mississippi Valley twice and formulated a flood control plan, but he had to put it on hold until Congress met again in the fall. In the meantime, Thompson approached him with a request from the conference executive committee for an audience with the House Flood Control Committee. Reid complied with the request upon the advice of the other committee members and scheduled preliminary meetings with the Chicago group on November 7. Thompson and eight hundred followers, complete with speeches, music and sing-a-longs, gathered at the Illinois Central Train Station for a festive send-off. Once in Washington, Big Bill and his entourage (aka Thompson's Army) continued in the same fashion in the ballroom of the Mayflower Hotel until the congressional meetings. Frank Reid quietly extended his authority throughout the first session following Thompson's initial fanfare, and by early December he became the group's leader.[246]

Competing flood control plans had already begun to emerge even before the Chicago conference. In May, Secretary Davis directed the Mississippi River Commission (MRC), which had had sole responsibility for the development of flood control policy since 1879, to prepare a flood control plan. Meanwhile, Jadwin, with support of the president, quietly set about drafting a plan of his own. He based his authority to do so on the Rivers and Harbors Act of January 21, 1927, which conferred upon the U.S. Army Corps of Engineers the right to make plans on practically all of the rivers of the United States for flood control. Jadwin planned to take advantage of the failure of the civilian MRC's levee system to widen the scope of his authority. He soon had 150 army engineers working on a rival plan for Mississippi River flood control, and as expected, Jadwin's report reflected Coolidge's fiscal conservatism. The MRC plan arrived in late September but never saw the light of day. Jadwin took many of the ideas presented in the report, rewriting them to reflect his ambitions and Coolidge's desire to cut costs, and gave them to the president on December 4.[247]

On December 6, Coolidge declared in his State of the Union address to Congress that the disaster-stricken Mississippi Valley should pay for part of the new flood control. Coolidge disappointed nearly everyone and created divisions within his own party that only served to unify opposition against him in the House Flood Control Committee. Two days later, Coolidge submitted Jadwin's report to Congress with his full support. Critics immediately attacked the plan for its use of "fuse-plugs" and dependence on local financial support. Governor John E. Marteneau of Arkansas, speaking as chair of the Tri-State Flood Control Committee, complained that local communities could not meet the additional financial requirements of the plan.[248]

Jadwin appeared twice in the House Flood Control hearings, only to anger the committee with condemnations of the MRC and his refusal to comment on the president's input on the proposed plan. On February 16, 1928, the Flood Control Committee introduced to the House what was known as the Reid Bill, authorizing an expenditure of $473 million with no local contribution requirements. Furthermore, it completely rejected Jadwin's ideas in favor of the creation of a seven-member Mississippi Valley Flood Control Commission. The commission would work on all major tributaries and was tasked very generally with implementing "such levees, controlled and regulated spillways, floodways, storage basins and reservoirs as in the judgment of the committee may be necessary to hold the flood crests."[249]

Coolidge denounced the proposal and threatened a veto to prevent a deficit unless Congress cut back on the costs. Republican Bertrand H. Snell of New York, chair of the House Rules Committee, remained friendly to the administration and refused to put the Reid Bill on the House calendar, resulting in a deadlock. The president hoped to work out a compromise measure in the Senate Commerce Committee, but members favored a more liberal view on local contributions. After pressure from fellow party members and a visit from Mayor Thompson, Coolidge reluctantly agreed to a compromise. Even so, he insisted on the creation of a commission to investigate the financial status of the Mississippi Valley after a year to determine whether or not communities could contribute any money to flood works.[250]

Missouri Democrat Harry Hawes, absent during the drafting, returned and insisted on reworking the bill to increase civilian involvement and do away with any local contributions. The new revisions gave Coolidge and Jadwin the opportunity to attack costs of the newly renamed Jones-Reid Bill. Members reached a compromise in May, and the bill passed in both Houses. Ransdell arranged for Coolidge to sign the bill in a ceremony surrounded by interested senators and representatives. Coolidge, contrary as ever, snubbed the ceremony and instead signed the bill while having lunch on May 15.[251]

The 1927 flood broke down the old ways of thinking about flooding, causing significant changes in policy and technology on both the national and local levels. Governing bodies, including the U.S. Army Corps of Engineers and local governments, had to rethink their approaches to flood control technology and disaster management as they came to terms with what appeared to be a new trend of catastrophic flooding. The enormity of the 1927 flood not only opened people's minds to the possibility of future super-floods, but it also left them with a sense of anxiety over how to deal with them.

The 1928 Flood Control Act, later known as the Mississippi River and Tributaries Project, changed flood control to meet the new challenges. Its creators designed all works on the basis of a worst-case scenario, a great hypothetical flood derived from examining historic rainfall and runoff patterns. The new plan included the incorporation of floodways to divert peak flows and hold down stages in the main channel above New Orleans, in the Tensas and Atchafalaya Basins and between Birds Eye and New Madrid, Missouri. It then provided backwater areas to divert peak flows from the river and store a portion of the floodwaters near the peak of the flood, resulting in reduced downstream stages.[252]

Memphians welcomed the new flood control measures in hopes that they would keep the city safe from future super-floods and protect their investments in surrounding areas. Memphis had much less damage than other communities throughout the Mississippi Valley; however, the 1927 flood caused concerns about the trend of worsening floods and the city's increased vulnerability. The people of Memphis and Shelby County had not experienced flood damage on this scale since 1913—and they certainly did not want to see it again. In addition, businessmen wanted greater flood control in order to protect their interests in surrounding plantations and secure the city's economy, which depended on the transportation and distribution of Mid-South farm goods and hardwood.[253]

Paine should have received a warm reception when he returned to Memphis. The city and the Mid-South would certainly benefit from the new flood control program brought about in part by the Chicago conference. Instead, he landed in the middle of a political maelstrom that damaged his public image and kept him from participating in conference activities.[254]

Ed Crump, former mayor and rising political boss, took advantage of the mayor's absence to launch an attack on his rival. Crump supported Paine in his last election, hoping to gain influence over him, but the mayor remained just out of Crump's control. Frustrated, Crump found a handpicked candidate named Watkins Overton to challenge Paine in the next election. The boss looked for a weakness in Paine and found it when federal agents arrested the notorious bootlegger John Bellomini and found a ledger containing an apparent list of bribes paid to local police officers.

No one bothered to notify Paine about the breaking scandal while he attended the Chicago flood control conference. To make matters worse, he did not find out from investigators, but rather from a newspaper reporter after he returned to Memphis. Paine sidestepped Attorney General Tyler McLain, a Crump supporter, and asked federal authorities to launch an investigation of the police department. He hoped the move would save face with voters, but it only further embarrassed him. Federal judge Harry Anderson refused, saying the case fell within the jurisdiction of the local attorney general.[255]

McLain made Paine appear uncooperative when he threatened to remove the mayor and Police Commissioner Thomas Allen unless they proceeded with an investigation. A report by the City Club, a local watchdog group, on July 30 further embarrassed Paine by stating that the mayor was wrong to not let the club initially examine the ledger and asserting that the police department was riddled with corruption. Commissioner Allen suspended forty-one police officers after a board charged them with inefficiency, incompetency and conduct unbecoming of an officer. However, Crump supporters found evidence that the officers actually received suspensions because they refused to support Paine's reelection. Attorney Charles Bryan pointed out the lack of proof that any of the officers ever received any pay-offs at all, and the trial board eventually declared the officers not guilty. Even so, the scandal left Paine politically weakened.[256]

Crump launched more attacks by courting defecting middle-class progressives along with disgruntled African Americans. Paine reneged on his 1923 promises of new streetlights, street paving, a new high school and the appointment of black firemen and police officers, costing him a great deal of support. The worst blow came when Bob Church, Wayman Wilkerson, George W. Lee and Dr. J.B. Martin established the West Tennessee Civic and Political League to oppose him.[257]

Paine, unlike Huey Long or Herbert Hoover, did not cash in on the political capital he earned from his efforts during the flood, opting instead to appeal to racist sentiment to try to win votes. Paine became desperate and tried to use fear to win back white voters by claiming that his opposition's victory would guarantee African American political ascendancy. He accused Crump of trying to rule through proxy and asserted that the election of his opponent Watkins Overton would mean an end to white control of Memphis, but few listened. Crump's handpicked candidate won the election and ushered in a new era of machine rule.[258]

EPILOGUE

I works on the levee, mama both night and day
I works on the levee, mama both night and day
I works so hard, to keep the water away
—Memphis Minnie and Kansas Joe McCoy, "When the Levee Breaks"[259]

Hoover said of the flood, "There was never such a calamity in our history." Indeed, the United States had never suffered such a widespread and long-lasting natural disaster as the Mississippi Valley Flood of 1927. The physical damage alone made a significant impact on the country; however, the effects did not end with the passing of the floodwaters. The political and social fallout from the handling of the flood forced a reticent federal government to finally take responsibility for flood control and incorporate new methods in its execution. The flood provided fodder for Hoover's political campaign, while at the same time exposing the depths of African Americans' plight in the South and hastening the exodus of many to the North.[260]

The Mississippi Valley Flood of 1927 tested the character of Memphians and Mid-Southerners like no other flood before. Local businessmen suffered the economic consequences of failed crops, damaged properties and the loss of field hands in the lowland areas affected by the flood. The more self-serving of them proved less than cooperative in relief efforts; however, the majority of Memphians rose to the occasion and gave aid to their neighbors in need. The city became a primary destination for refugees in need of immediate shelter and assistance, and Memphians eagerly responded. They donated, volunteered and risked their lives to rescue those stranded by the flood.

The local government made an impressive showing during the flood as well. Crews bolstered levees, and the fairgrounds transformed into the region's best-equipped refugee camp. Mayor Paine made every effort to cooperate with Hoover and the Red Cross by using the city's resources to provide for refugees escaping the flood's devastation. He even participated in the movement to force new federal flood control, while inadvertently stumbling into a political quagmire.

The Mid-South took the brunt of the flood in the first weeks of the disaster, and the position of Memphis as the region's distribution center made it an excellent choice as the Red Cross headquarters. Supplies, money and personnel poured into the city for relief agencies. The city had not played such a role in regional affairs since the Civil War, and the lessons learned from the experience provided a valuable blueprint for handling future disasters.

Even with the change of guard, flood control remained a priority in Memphis after 1927. Mayor Overton personally met with President Hoover to secure federal funding of flood control for Memphis. However, a certain anxiety persisted. Flooding continued to worsen with continued deforestation, making the possibility of another disaster very likely. In addition, no one knew for a fact that the new flood control measures would work in the event of another super flood. Memphians kept a careful watch on the Mississippi River, ever mindful of its potential for destruction. They knew that one day it would once again lash out at its handlers like a caged but untamed animal. A decade later, the river would rise again, but this time Memphis would be ready.[261]

NOTES

INTRODUCTION

1. Charley Patton, *Charlie Patton: Founder of the Delta Blues: 1929–1934*.
2. Risk Management Solutions, Inc., *The 1927 Great Mississippi Flood: 80-Year Retrospective* (Newark, CA: Risk Management Solutions, Inc., 2007), 12.
3. *Time*, "Catastrophe: Deluge," May 2, 1927.

CHAPTER 1

4. Douglas Bukowski, *Big Bill Thompson, Chicago, and the Politics of Image* (Chicago: University of Illinois Press, 1998), 206.
5. Matthew T. Pearcy, "After the Flood: A History of the 1928 Flood Control Act," *Journal of the Illinois State Historical Society* (Summer 2002): 175; *Time*, "In Chicago," April 18, 1927.
6. Bukowski, *Big Bill Thompson*, 191; *Commercial Appeal* (Memphis) "Mayor Thompson's Party Travels by Water and Rail," April 20, 1927.
7. *Commercial Appeal*, "Mayor Thompson and Party Due Here Today," April 21, 1927; *Commercial Appeal*, "Mayor Thompson's Party Travels by Water and Rail," 8; Pearcy, "After the Flood," 172.
9. Pearcy, "After the Flood," 172; *Memphis Evening Appeal*, "Levee Menaced by Boat Waves Engineer Says," April 20, 1927; *Commercial Appeal*, "Chicago Mayor and Party Donate $1000," April 22, 1927.
10. Letter from William Hale Thompson to Rowlett Paine, April 21, 1927, Rowlett Paine Collection, Memphis-Shelby County Room, Memphis Public Library & Information Center, Box 13; *Commercial Appeal*, "Chicago Mayor and Party Donate $1000," April 22, 1927.

11. *Commercial Appeal*, "Chicago Mayor and Party Donate $1000," April 22, 1927; U.S. Army Corps of Engineers, Mississippi Valley Division/Mississippi River Commission, *75th Anniversary of the Great Flood of 1927* (March 12, 2002).

12. John M. Barry, "After the Deluge: As Hurricane Katrina Made Clear, the Lessons of the Mississippi Flood of 1927 (Which Made Herbert Hoover President) Have Yet to Be Learned," *Smithsonian* (November 2005): 114–17.

13. Ibid.; Floyd M. Clay, *A Century on the Mississippi: A History of the Memphis District U.S. Army Corps of Engineers, 1876–1981* (Memphis: U.S. Army Corps of Engineers, 1986), 83.

14. Pete Daniel, *Deep'n as It Come: The 1927 Mississippi River Flood* (Fayetteville: University of Arkansas Press, 1996), 3–8.

15. Bette B. Tilly, "Memphis and the Mississippi Valley Flood of 1927," *West Tennessee Historical Society Papers* 24 (1970): 41.

16. Risk Management Solutions, Inc., *The 1927 Great Mississippi Flood*, 3; Clay, *A Century on the Mississippi*, 83.

17. *Memphis Evening Appeal*, "Memphis Crest of 41 Feet Is Now Probable," April 4, 1927.

18. *Memphis Evening Appeal*, "Burke's Levee Cracks Under Heavy Strain," April 7, 1927.

19. Barry, "After the Deluge," 186; *Memphis Evening Appeal*, "Flood Reports Are Regarded as Favorable," April 8, 1927.

20. *Memphis Evening Appeal*, "Burke's Levee Cracks Under Heavy Strain," April 7, 1927; *Memphis Evening Appeal*, "2 Floors, Stock Crash Through; Rest in Water," April 9, 1927; Barry, "After the Deluge," 186; *Memphis Evening Appeal*, "Army Fights at Columbus to Save Town," April 9, 1927.

21. *Memphis Evening Appeal*, "400 Battle to Repair Breaks in Flooded Area," April 11, 1927.

22. *Memphis Evening Appeal*, "Stage of 42.3 Hits Memphis; Levees Taxed," April 12, 1927; *Memphis Evening Appeal*, "Desert Towns as Dykes Yield to High Water," April 14, 1927.

23. Risk Management Solutions, Inc., *The 1927 Great Mississippi Flood*; *Memphis Evening Appeal*, "Issue Warning to Prepare for Huge Overflow," April 15, 1927.

24. U.S. Army Corps of Engineers, *75th Anniversary of the Great Flood of 1927*.

25. Gerald M. Capers, *The Mississippi River: Before and After Mark Twain* (Hicksville, NY: Exposition Press, 1977), 77; U.S. Army Corps of Engineers, Mississippi River Commission, *Improvement of the Lower Mississippi River and Tributaries: 1931–1972* (Vicksburg: Mississippi River Commission, 1972), 1–2; Kevin R. Kosar, "Disaster Response and Appointment of a Recovery Czar: The Executive Branch's Response to the Flood of 1927," *Congressional Research Service (CRS) Reports and Issue Briefs*, 2005.

26. Tilly, "Memphis and the Mississippi Valley Flood of 1927," 52.

CHAPTER 2

27. Memphis Minnie, *Queen of the Blues*.

28. *Commercial Appeal*, "Cemeteries Become Living Bivouacs; Refugees in Boxcars Flooded Out; Railmen Marooned Fight Flood," April 21, 1927.

29. *Memphis Evening Appeal*, "Wiped Out by Rushing Water," April 20, 1927.

30. *Commercial Appeal*, "Forrest City Is Haven for Flood Refugees," April 21, 1927; *Commercial Appeal*, "Clarendon Wrecked by Waters of Flood," May 6, 1927.

31. Nancy Hendricks, "Flood of 1927," *Encyclopedia of Arkansas History and Culture* (Little Rock: Central Arkansas Library System, 2009).

32. Ibid.

33. Ibid.

34. Donna Brewer Jackson, "Levees and Drainage Districts," *Encyclopedia of Arkansas History and Culture* (Little Rock: Central Arkansas Library, 2009).

35. *Memphis Evening Appeal*, "Stage of 42.3 Hits Memphis; Levees Taxed," April 12, 1927; *Memphis Evening Appeal*, "Flood Equal to 1913 Coming Down," April 15, 1927.

36. *Memphis Evening Appeal*, "Flood Equal to 1913 Coming Down," April 15, 1927; *Memphis Evening Appeal*, "Waters Sweep Across 175,000 Acres of Land," April 16, 1927; *Memphis Evening Appeal*, "Floods Sweep 3,000,000 Acres of Delta Land," April 18, 1927; *Memphis Evening Appeal*, "Flood Heads Toward Marked Tree Section," April 20, 1927; *Commercial Appeal*, "The Situation at a Glance," April 22, 1927; *Commercial Appeal*, "Water Six Feet Deep in Dermott Streets," April 27, 1927; *Commercial Appeal*, "Desperate Situation Found Arkansas City," April 28, 1927; *Commercial Appeal*, "Hills Offer Safety to Thousands Caught in Flooded Valley," April 28, 1927.

37. *Memphis Evening Appeal*, "Bus Escapes as Bridge Goes Out," April 15, 1927; *Memphis Evening Appeal*, "Town in Arkansas Is Washed Away," April 20, 1927; *Memphis Evening Appeal*, "Thousand Flee as Levee Breaks," April 19, 1927.

38. *Time*, "Deluge," May 2, 1927; *Memphis Evening Appeal*, "Mellwood Girl Falls Off Porch, Drowns in Flood," April 6, 1927; *Memphis Evening Appeal*, "Missing Girl, Boy Believed Flood Victims," April 18, 1927; *Memphis Evening Appeal*, "Floods Sweep 3,000,000 Acres of Delta Land," April 18, 1927; *Memphis Evening Appeal*, "Thousand Flee as Levee Breaks," April 19, 1927; *Commercial Appeal*, "Little Rock Almost Cut Off from the World," April 21, 1927.

39. *Memphis Evening Appeal*, "Flood Equal to 1913 Coming Down," April 15, 1927; *Memphis Evening Appeal*, "Town in Arkansas Is Washed Away," April 20, 1927; *Commercial Appeal*, "Viaduct Control Is Conference Subject," April 29, 1927.

40. *Memphis Evening Appeal*, "Thousand Flee as Levee Breaks," April 19, 1927; *Commercial Appeal*, "Mercury Down 36 Degrees," April 22, 1927; *Commercial Appeal*, "Suffering Is Acute Around Pine Bluff," April 22, 1927.

41. *Commercial Appeal*, "Refugees Flow In," April 21, 1927; *Memphis Evening Appeal*, "Refugees Flocking into Marianna, Ark.," April 19, 1927; *Memphis Evening Appeal*, "Marianna Shelters 3,000 of Destitute," April 23, 1927; *Memphis Evening Appeal*, "Steamers Rescue Brickeys People; Five Are Drowned," April 25, 1927.

42. *Commercial Appeal*, "Forrest City Is Haven for Flood Refugees," April 21, 1927; *Commercial Appeal*, "10,929 Refugees in Camp at Forrest City, Making It Largest in Disaster," April 10, 1927.

43. *Commercial Appeal*, "82,250 Flood Refugees Reported in Arkansas," May 4, 1927; *Time*, "Deluge," May 2, 1927.

44. *Commercial Appeal*, "The Situation at a Glance," April 22, 1927; *Memphis Evening Appeal*, "High Water Stops Memphis Students," April 15, 1927; *Commercial Appeal*, "Heavy Guard Keeps Vigil at Reelfoot," April 21, 1927; *New York Times*, "Flood Is Spreading, 200,000 Destitute," April 26, 1927.

45. *Commercial Appeal*, "Greenville Flooded When City Levee Is Topped by Torrent," April 22, 1927; *Commercial Appeal*, "Farm Hands Perish at Scott Crevasse," April 22, 1927; *Commercial Appeal*, "Scott Break Went in at Bottom of Levee," April 22, 1927.

46. *Memphis Evening Appeal*, "Man Sees Wife Four Children Sink to Death," April 23, 1927; *Memphis Evening Appeal*, "Man's Wife Rescued but Children Lost," April 26, 1927.

47. *Memphis Evening Appeal*, "Cold, Half-Starved, Thirsty, Greenville's Remnant Waits Aid," April 25, 1927; *Memphis Evening Appeal*, "Pinky Took Long Chances—But He Got the Pictures," April 25, 1927.

48. *Commercial Appeal*, "Federal Help Sought After Vast Area Is Threatened by Flood," April 22, 1927.

49. Ibid.

50. *Memphis Evening Appeal*, "Cleveland, Miss., Pleads for Bedding for Victims," April 25, 1927; *Memphis Evening Appeal*, "Fleet of Boats Takes Refugees to Beeson Camp," April 23, 1927.

51. Princella Wilkerson Nowell, "The Flood of 1927 and Its Impact in Greenville, Mississippi," *Mississippi Historical Society*, March 2006, http://mshistorynow.mdah.state.ms.us/articles/230/the-flood-of-1927-and-its-impact-in-greenville-mississippi.

52. *Commercial Appeal*, "Food Hogs Halted in Greenville Flood," April 29, 1927; *Memphis Evening Appeal*, "Memphis Sends Fire Pumper to Aid Greenville," April 26, 1927; *Commercial Appeal*, "Hills Offer Safety to Thousands Caught in Flooded Valley," April 28, 1927; Commercial Appeal, "Water Receding," May 18, 1927.

53. *Commercial Appeal*, "Hills Offer Safety to Thousands Caught in Flooded Valley," April 28, 1927; *Commercial Appeal*, "Food Hogs Halted in Greenville Flood," April 29, 1927; *Time*, "Flood Continued," May 16, 1927; *Commercial Appeal*, "Flood Five Feet Deep in Yazoo City Streets," May 3, 1927.

54. *Commercial Appeal*, "Y&MV Is Winning Costly Flood Battle," May 6, 1927; *Commercial Appeal*, "More Troops Called to Work in the Delta," April 28, 1927; *Commercial Appeal*, "Vigilance Committee Routs Labor Agents at Yazoo City Camp," May 6, 1927.

55. Ibid.

56. *Commercial Appeal*, "Courage of Hannibal Shown in Flood Stricken Delta," May 22, 1927.

57. William Howard, "Richard Wright's Flood Stories and the Great Mississippi River Flood of 1927: Social and Historical Backgrounds," *Southern Literary Journal* 16 (Spring 1984): 44.

58. Pete Daniel, *The Shadow of Slavery: Peonage in the South, 1901–1969* (Chicago: University of Illinois, 1990), 151; Robin Spencer, "Contested Terrain: The Mississippi Flood of 1927 and the Struggle to Control Black Labor," *Journal of Negro History* 79, no. 2 (Spring 1994): 171–81.

59. Spencer, "Contested Terrain," 171–81; Howard, "Richard Wright's Flood Stories," 44.

60. Hendricks, "Flood of 1927"; Daniel, *Shadow of Slavery*, 153–54.

61. Spencer, "Contested Terrain," 171–81.

62. Hendricks, "Flood of 1927"; Spencer, "Contested Terrain," 171–81.

63. John Barton Payne (Red Cross Chairman), "The Final Report of the Colored Advisory Commission Appointed to Cooperate with the American National Red Cross and the President's Committee on Relief Work in the Mississippi Valley Flood Disaster of 1927," Public Broadcasting Service, http://www.pbs.org/wgbh/americanexperience/features/primary-resources/flood-cacr/.

64. Daniel, *Shadow of Slavery*, 153–54.

65. William Edward Leuchtenburg, *Herbert Hoover* (New York: Henry Holt and Company, 2009), 69.

66. *Time*, "Flood Aftermath," August 8, 1927.

67. Barry, "After the Deluge," 114–17.

68. Daniel, *Shadow of Slavery*, 152.

CHAPTER 3

69. *Commercial Appeal*, "Refugees Adapt Themselves to Routine of Daily Camp Life," April 28, 1927.

70. Ibid.

71. Ibid.

72. *Commercial Appeal*, "One of the World's Most Staggering Tragedies, Says R.C. Chairman," May 2, 1927.

73. Ibid.

74. *Memphis Evening Appeal*, "Refugee Camp Is Opened Here," April 20, 1927.

75. *Commercial Appeal*, "Memphis Holds Out Arms to Sufferers," April 22, 1927.

76. *Commercial Appeal*, "Care for Refugees," April 21, 1927.

77. *Commercial Appeal*, "Mayor Paine Speeds Work at Relief Camp," April 21, 1927; *Memphis Evening Appeal*, "Flood Victims from Arkansas Brought Here," April 19, 1927; *Memphis Evening Appeal*, "Col. Waring Issues Fair Grounds Rules," April 25, 1927.

78. MemphisHistory.com, "Rowlett Paine," http://www.memphishistory. org/Politics/TheMayorsofMemphis/Biographies3/RowlettPaine/ tabid/252/Default.aspx.

79. *Commercial Appeal*, "Legion and Red Cross Start Refugee Camp," April 20, 1927; *Commercial Appeal*, "Mayor Paine Speeds Work at Relief Camp," April 21, 1927; *Memphis Evening Appeal*, "Memphis Heeds Cry for Boats and Provisions," April 23, 1927.

80. *Memphis Evening Appeal*, "Viaduct Refugee Quarters Set Up," April 23, 1927; *Memphis Evening Appeal*, "Eight Families Flee Hughes Flood Area," April 25, 1927.

81. *Commercial Appeal*, "Army Tents Sent Here from Atlanta," April 21, 1927; *Memphis Evening Appeal*, "Refugee Camp Is Opened Here," April 20, 1927; *Memphis Evening Appeal*, "Flood Victims from Arkansas Brought Here," April 19, 1927.

82. *Commercial Appeal*, "Legion and Red Cross Start Refugee Camp," April 20, 1927; *Memphis Evening Appeal*, "Flood Victims from Arkansas Brought Here," April 19, 1927; *Memphis Evening Appeal* "Refugee Town Here Taking on Normal Aspect," April 23, 1927.

83. *Memphis Evening Appeal*, "Refugee Town Here Taking on Normal Aspect," April 23, 1927, 7; *Memphis Evening Appeal*, "Col. Waring Issues Fair Grounds Rules," April 25, 1927.

84. *Memphis Evening Appeal*, "Shelby County Court Asked to Attend Dance," April 18, 1927; *Commercial Appeal*, "Memphis Women to Be Filmed This Afternoon," May 6, 1927; *Commercial Appeal*, "Local Legionnaires Win National Thanks," May 13, 1927.

85. *Commercial Appeal*, "Relief Among Negroes," April 22, 1927.

86. *Commercial Appeal*, "Plan Entertainment for Flood Refugees," April 29, 1927; *Memphis Evening Appeal*, "Refugee Town Here Taking on Normal Aspect," April 23, 1927; *Memphis Evening Appeal*, "D'Molay Boys' Band Plays for Refugees," April 25, 1927; *Commercial Appeal*, "New Bry's Give Third of a Ton of Candy to White and Negro Refugee Children in Camp," May 3, 1927.

87. *Commercial Appeal*, "Flood Refugee Camps Now Shelter 158,000," May 4, 1927.

88. *Commercial Appeal*, "Turner Orders Toll Off Flood Refugees," April 22, 1927; *Memphis Evening Appeal*, "Meanest Thief Steals Refugees Wagon, Mules," April 23, 1927; *Commercial Appeal*, "Refugees Not Required to Agree to Pay for Aid," May 3, 1927.

89. *Commercial Appeal*, "Crevasses in Levees Are Ordered Closed," May 19, 1927.

90. *Commercial Appeal*, "Close Hickman Camp," May 15, 1927; *Commercial Appeal*, "Ripley Refugees Gone," May 15, 1927; *Commercial Appeal*, "Belzoni's Refugees Return by Carloads," May 17, 1927; *Commercial Appeal*, "Kilpatrick Directs Rehabilitation Work," May 27, 1927.

91. *Commercial Appeal*, "1,365 Refugees in Camp," May 5, 1927; *Commercial Appeal*, "Prisoners Will Help," May 13, 1927; *Commercial Appeal*, "Celebration Planned Fairgrounds Opening," May 28, 1927.

92. Tilly, "Memphis and the Mississippi Valley Flood of 1927," 53.

Chapter 4

93. *Memphis Evening Appeal*, "Relief Cruise in St. Francis Flood Related," April 25, 1927.

94. Ibid.

95. Ibid.

96. Ibid.

97. *Memphis Evening Appeal*, "Agencies Here Organized in Flood Relief," April 18, 1927, 2.

98. *New York Times*, "Red Cross Is Succoring 80,000 Destitute as Flood Spreads Over 9,000 Square Miles; Property Loss May Reach $1,000,000," April 25, 1927; Russell C. Jacobs, "Donald H. Connolly," *Arlington National Cemetery*, http://www.arlingtoncemetery.net/dhconnolly.htm.

99. *Commercial Appeal*, "Memphis Will Become Flood Relief Center," April 21, 1927; *Commercial Appeal*, "Army Corps Sets Up Central Relief Base," April 22, 1927.

100. *Commercial Appeal*, "Choctaw Goes on Trip," April 22, 1927; *Commercial Appeal*, "Suffering Is Acute Around Pine Bluff," April 22,

1927; *Memphis Evening Appeal*, "Memphis Heeds Cry for Boats and Provisions," April 23, 1927.

101. *New York Times*, "Radio Appeals Aid Red Cross Flood Drive," June 5, 1927; *Commercial Appeal*, "WMC Flood Radiograms Only News Source for Towns in Flood Section," April 22, 1927; *Memphis Evening Appeal*, "Useless Telephone Calls Hurt Relief," April 23, 1927; *New York Times*, "Thousands in Peril Awaiting Rescue," April 27, 1927.

102. *Commercial Appeal*, "Organize River Craft Under Col. Spalding," April 27, 1927.

103. *New York Times*, "Thousands in Peril Awaiting Rescue," April 27, 1927; *Memphis Evening Appeal*, "Two Cincinnati Boats Ordered to Flood Area," April 26, 1927; *Commercial Appeal*, "Many Boats on Rescue," April 29, 1927.

104. *Commercial Appeal*, "Watercraft Division Watches Weak Levees," May 4, 1927; *Commercial Appeal*, "Organize River Craft Under Col. Spalding," April 27, 1927; *New York Times*, "Donations Pour in for Flood Relief," April 26, 1927.

105. *Memphis Evening Appeal*, "Chief City of South Periled by Flood Water," April 26, 1927; *Commercial Appeal*, "Levee at South Bend Not Broken, Report," April 27, 1927.

106. *Commercial Appeal*, "Greenville Flooded When City Levee Is Topped by Torrent," April 22, 1927; *Commercial Appeal*, "Farm Hands Perish at Scott Crevasse," April 22, 1927; *Memphis Evening Appeal*, "Memphis Heeds Cry for Boats and Provisions," April 23, 1927; *Commercial Appeal*, "Boats to Greenville," April 22, 1927; *Memphis Press Scimitar*, "Louis Leroy," May 10, 1944; *Commercial Appeal*, "Louis Leroy," June 29, 1980.

107. *Commercial Appeal*, Photograph caption, May 8, 1927; *Commercial Appeal*, "Leroy-Newsum Crew Makes Memphis Port," May 7, 1927;

108. *Memphis Evening Appeal*, "Dyke Goes Out at South Bend; Adds to Flood," April 25, 1927; *Commercial Appeal*, "Memphis Cruisers Are Aiding," April 30, 1927; *Commercial Appeal*, "Leroy-Newsum Crew Makes Memphis Port," May 7, 1927.

109. *Commercial Appeal*, "Leroy-Newsum Crew Makes Memphis Port," May 7, 1927.

110. *Time*, "Deluge," May 2, 1927.

111. Clay, *A Century on the Mississippi*, 86.

112. *Commercial Appeal*, "Eighteen Lost When Boat Is Drawn into Levee Break, Report," April 22, 1927.

113. *Memphis Evening Appeal*, "Knowlton Flood Victims Taken to Safe Points," April 23, 1927; *Memphis Evening Appeal*, "Hope Abandoned for 1927 Crops in Flooded Area," April 25, 1927.

114. *Commercial Appeal*, "Labors in Rescue Work Made Widows of These Women and Orphans of Children," April 29, 1927; *Commercial Appeal*, "Fund for Widows of Flood Gets $116," May 6, 1927; *Commercial Appeal*, "Prepare to Settle All Pelican Claims," May 13, 1927.

115. *Commercial Appeal*, "Four Bodies Located," May 4, 1927; *Commercial Appeal*, "Eleven More Bodies Found at Knowlton," May 6, 1927;

116. *Commercial Appeal*, "Fund to Aid Sisters Widowed by Flood Is Growing Slowly," May 5, 1927; *Commercial Appeal*, "Fund for Widows of Flood Gets $116," May 6, 1927; *Commercial Appeal* (Memphis), "Prepare to Settle All Pelican Claims," May 13, 1927; *Commercial Appeal*, "Four Pelican Victims Sent Here for Burial," May 8, 1927; *Commercial Appeal*, "Pelican Victim Rites," May 9, 1927.

117. *Commercial Appeal*, "Freight Train Still Marooned in Waters," May 3, 1927.

118. *Memphis Evening Appeal*, "New Break Near New Madrid to Peril Vast Area," April 20, 1927.

119. *Memphis Evening Appeal*, "Railway Service Here Slowed Up by Flood," April 18, 1927; *Memphis Evening Appeal*, "Long Detour Is Last Link to Southwest," April 19, 1927.

120. *Memphis Evening Appeal*, "Three Lines to Arkansas Left Minus Service," April 20, 1927; *Commercial Appeal*, "Rotarian Convention Halted by the Flood," April 20, 1927; *Commercial Appeal*, "Little Rock Almost Cut Off from the World," April 21, 1927; *Memphis Evening Appeal*, "Train Service from Paragould Resumed," April 20, 1927; *Commercial Appeal*, "Forrest City Is Haven for Flood Refugees," April 21, 1927.

121. *Memphis Evening Appeal*, "Freight Routing Subordinate to Floods-ICC," April 23, 1927; *Commercial Appeal*, "Little Rock Almost Cut Off from the World," April 21, 1927; *Commercial Appeal*, "Red Cross Asks Aid for Flood Victims," April 21, 1927; *Commercial Appeal*, "Cemeteries Become Living Bivouacs; Refugees in Boxcars Flooded Out; Railmen Marooned Fight Flood," April 21, 1927; *Commercial Appeal*, "Pullmans for Refugees," April 28, 1927.

122. *Commercial Appeal*, "Frisco to Resume Daylight Service," April 28, 1927; *Commercial Appeal*, "Railroad Operations Near Pre-Flood Basis," May 5, 1927; *Commercial Appeal*, "Restore Memphis-Helena Service on M.P. Monday," May 15, 1927; *Commercial Appeal*, "Y&MV Trains to Resume Service," May 25, 1927; Daniel, *Deep'n as It Come*, 193.

123. *Commercial Appeal*, "Epic Stories of Railroading Produced in Fights Flood," May 31, 1927;

124. *Commercial Appeal*, "Ace of Aces Remains Here After Accident," May 15, 1927;

125. *Commercial Appeal*, "Great Italian Ace Is to Arrive Here Friday," May 12, 1927; *Commercial Appeal*, "Ace of Aces Remains Here After Accident," May 15, 1927.

126. Ibid.

127. *Commercial Appeal*, "Federal Help Sought After Vast Area Is Threatened by Flood," April 22, 1927; *Commercial Appeal*, "Watercraft Division Watches Weak Levees," May 4, 1927.

128. Clay, *A Century on the Mississippi*, 85; *New York Times*, "City of Tents Three Miles Long Crown Levee at Greenville," April 25, 1927; *Time*, "Deluge," May 2, 1927; *Memphis Evening Appeal*, "Engineer to Inspect Levees with Plane," April 18, 1927.

129. *Memphis Evening Appeal*, "Chief City of South Periled by Flood Water," April 26, 1927; *Commercial Appeal*, "Levee at South Bend Not Broken, Report," April 27, 1927; *Commercial Appeal*, "Two Big Seaplanes for Red Cross Help," April 28, 1927; *Commercial Appeal*, "Order Relief Boats to Belzoni Section," April 28, 1927; *New York Times*, "Flying 48 Planes for Flood Relief," May 5, 1927.

130. *Commercial Appeal*, "Offer Hoover Airplane," April 27, 1927; *Memphis Evening Appeal*, "Planes at New Bry's Will See Flood Service," April 23, 1927.

131. *Commercial Appeal*, "Airport, Playground to be Opened Sunday," May 5, 1927; *Commercial Appeal*, "Sitting Made in the Air," May 19, 1927.

132. *Memphis Evening Appeal*, "Air Mail Service," April 25, 1927.

133. *Commercial Appeal*, "Urges Memphis to Establish Airport," April 27, 1927.

134. *Memphis Evening Appeal*, "400 Battle to Repair Breaks in Flooded Area," April 11, 1927; *Commercial Appeal*, "Lieut. Omlie Due Today," April 22, 1927; *Commercial Appeal*, "Watercraft Division Watches Weak Levees," May 4, 1927.

135. *Commercial Appeal*, "Head of Relief Dies in Plane Crash," May 31, 1927.

CHAPTER 5

136. Diane Holloway and Bob Cheney, *American History in Song: Lyrics from 1900 to 1945* (Lincoln, NE: iUniverse, 2001), 253.

137. Telegram from Secretary Hoover's assistant George E. Ackerson to Paine regarding using Memphis as a Red Cross headquarters, Rowlett Paine Collection, Box 13; *Memphis Evening Appeal*, "Memphis Made Headquarters for Red Cross," April 23, 1927.

138. *Memphis Evening Appeal*, "Red Cross Help for 200,000 Is Needed— Hoover," April 25, 1927; *Memphis Evening Appeal*, "Hoover, Here, Gets on the Job Early; Eats Bacon and Eggs," April 25, 1927.

139. Ibid.

140. Turner Catledge, *My Life and the Times* (New York: Harper and Row, 1971) 47–48.

141. Ibid.

142. *Memphis Evening Appeal*, "Red Cross Help for 200,000 Is Needed—Hoover," April 25, 1927; *Memphis Evening Appeal*, "Hoover, Here, Gets on the Job Early; Eats Bacon and Eggs," April 25, 1927; Catledge, *My Life and the Times*, 48.

143. *New York Times*, "Flood Hits More Towns; 200,000 Are Now Destitute; $1,234,000 Given for Relief," April 26, 1927; *Memphis Evening Appeal*, "Red Cross Help for 200,000 is Needed—Hoover," April 25, 1927; *Memphis Evening Appeal*, "Hoover, Here, Gets on the Job Early; Eats Bacon and Eggs," April 25, 1927.

144. *Memphis Evening Appeal*, "Lesson from the Flood," April 25, 1927.

145. *Commercial Appeal*, "Nation Turns to Hoover in Time of National Disaster," May 9, 1927.

146. Kevin R. Kosar, "The Executive Branch's Response to the Flood of 1927," *History News Network*, October 31, 2005, http://hnn.us/articles/17255.html.

147. John M. Barry, *Rising Tide: The Great Mississippi Flood of 1927 and How It Changed America* (New York: Simon & Schuster, 1998), 274.

148. *Memphis Evening Appeal*, "Red Cross Help for 200,000 Is Needed—Hoover," April 25, 1927; *Memphis Evening Appeal*, "Hoover, Here, Gets on the Job Early; Eats Bacon and Eggs," April 25, 1927; *Memphis Evening Appeal*, "Chief City of South Periled by Flood Water," April 26, 1927; *Memphis Evening Appeal*, "Appoint Chiefs River and Rail for Emergency," April 26, 1927.

149. Dorothy Abbott, *Mississippi Writers: Reflections of Childhood and Youth* (Jackson: University Press of Mississippi, 1988), 406; M. Susan Klopfer, Fred Klopfer and Barry Klopfer, *Where Rebels Roost: Mississippi Civil Right Revisited* (M. Susan Klopfer, 2005), 153.

150. *Commercial Appeal*, "Hoover Will Spend Millions in South After Flood Over," April 27, 1927.

151. Catledge, *My Life and the Times*, 51.

152. Ibid., 50.

153. *Commercial Appeal*, "Hoover at Greenville Surveys Flooded City," April 27, 1927; *Commercial Appeal*, "7,931 Refugees Taken to Four Guard Camps," April 27, 1927.

154. Kosar, "Disaster Response and Appointment of a Recovery Czar."

155. *Commercial Appeal*, "Couch Head of Relief in Flooded Arkansas," May 1, 1927.

156. *Commercial Appeal*, "Hoover Paints Vivid Picture of Havoc in Mississippi Valley," May 1, 1927.

157. Ibid.

158. Ibid.

159. Kosar, "The Executive Branch's Response to the Flood of 1927."
160. *Commercial Appeal*, "Coolidge Makes Plea for $5,000,000 More to Aid Flood Victims," May 3, 1927.
161. *Commercial Appeal*, "Hoover Will Speak on Relief Program," May 28, 1927.
162. Kosar, "Disaster Response and Appointment of a Recovery Czar"; Pearcy, "After the Flood," 174; *Time Magazine*, "Deluge," May 2, 1927.
163. *Commercial Appeal*, "Small Boats Race Over Delta Ocean on Mercy Missions," April 29, 1927; *Commercial Appeal*, "Coolidge Makes Plea for $5,000,000 More to Aid Flood Victims," May 3, 1927.
164. *Commercial Appeal*, "Coolidge Will Send Engineers to South," May 4, 1927; *Commercial Appeal*, "Aid from Coolidge Asked in Arkansas," April 29, 1927; *Commercial Appeal*, "Coolidge Is Asked to Call Special Session," May 5, 1927.
165. *Commercial Appeal*, "Will Ask Congress for Drainage Help," May 26, 1927; *Commercial Appeal*, "Flood Relief Session Urged by Cotton Men," May 26, 1927.
166. Barry, *Rising Tide*, 366–69.
167. Daniel, *Deep'n as It Come*, 186.
168. *Commercial Appeal*, "Memphis Banks Asked to Aid Rehabilitation," May 20, 1927; *Commercial Appeal*, "Second Relief Appeal Broadcast by Crosby," May 21, 1927.
169. *Commercial Appeal*, "Memphis Will Raise $200,000 for South," May 25, 1927; Daniel, *Deep'n as It Come*, 188.
170. *Commercial Appeal*, "Memphis Will Raise $200,000 for South," May 25, 1927.
171. *Commercial Appeal*, "Complete Plans for Raising Flood Relief," May 28, 1927.
172. *Commercial Appeal*, "Memphis Will Raise Rehabilitation Fund," May 29, 1927; *Commercial Appeal*, "Rehabilitation Fund Is Over Fourth Raised," May 31, 1927; *Commercial Appeal*, "Workers on the Job for Rehabilitation Fund," May 30, 1927.
173. *Commercial Appeal*, "Memphis Will Raise Rehabilitation Fund," May 29, 1927.
174. Pearcy, "After the Flood," 189.
175. Kelman, *A River and Its City*, 187.

Chapter 6

176. *Commercial Appeal*, "Palace Flood Benefit Gets City's Sanction," April 22, 1927.
177. Telegrams and money transfer from crew of *Memphis* to Mayor Paine, Rowlett Paine Collection, Box 13; *Commercial Appeal*, "Cable Mayor Paine $200 for Flood Aid," April 20, 1927.

178. Papers of Henry E. Lackey, Operational Archives Branch, Naval Historical Center, Washington, D.C., November 2006, http://www.history.navy.mil/ar/lima/lackey_he.htm.

179. *Commercial Appeal*, "Cable Mayor Paine $200 for Flood Aid," April 20, 1927.

180. See various telegrams and letters of introduction from Paine, Rowlett Paine Collection, Box 13.

181. *New York Times*, "Nation Swift to Aid," April 25, 1927; *New York Times*, "Smith Asks People of the State to Aid Flood Sufferers," April 27, 1927; *New York Times*, "Flood Fund Here Reaches $140,474," April 26, 1927; *Commercial Appeal*, "Gotham's Contribution to Flood Relief Fund Passes $1,000,000 Mark," May 4, 1927; *Commercial Appeal*, "Belgium Sympathizes," April 29, 1927; *Commercial Appeal*, "Coolidge Makes Plea for $5,000,000 More to Aid Flood Victims," May 3, 1927; *Commercial Appeal*, "French Red Cross Donates to Fund for Flood Relief," May 5, 1927.

182. *Commercial Appeal*, "More Than $1200 in for Flood Sufferers," April 22, 1927; *Commercial Appeal*, "Boy Scouts Pledge Help," April 22, 1927; *Commercial Appeal*, "Public Responds to Plea for Clothing," April 22, 1927; *Memphis Evening Appeal*, "Memphis Heeds Cry for Boats and Provisions," April 23, 1927.

183. *Memphis Evening Appeal*, "Theaters Asked to Aid," April 26, 1927; Commercial Appeal, "Coleen Moore Pays $1,000 for Seat at Benefit for Flood," April 28, 1927; Robert Springer, *Nobody Knows Where the Blues Came From: Lyrics and History* (Oxford: University of Mississippi Press, 2006), 12.

184. *Commercial Appeal*, "Palace Flood Benefit Gets City's Sanction," April 22, 1927.

185. *Memphis Evening Appeal*, "Big Show Sunday at Loew's State for Flood Relief," April 23, 1927; *Memphis Evening Appeal*, "$3,620 Is Raised in Theaters for Refugee Relief," April 25, 1927.

186. *Commercial Appeal*, "Secretary Hoover to Speak at Auditorium," April 27, 1927; *Commercial Appeal*, "Big Crowd Expected at Benefit Concert," May 1, 1927.

187. Letter to Commissioner Thomas Allen from Rowlett Paine, May 18, 1927, Rowlett Paine Collection, Box 13.

188. *Memphis Evening Appeal*, "Sunday Movie Bill Passed by Senate," April 23, 1927.

189. Ibid.; *Commercial Appeal*, "Senate Over-rides Peay on Movie Bill, House, However, Refuses to Pass Over Veto," April 28, 1927.

190. *Commercial Appeal*, "Give Flood Benefit Tonight at Pantages," May 1, 1927; *Commercial Appeal*, "Palace Show Benefit of Refugees," May 6, 1927.

191. *Commercial Appeal*, "Salon Circle to Aid," April 22, 1927; *Commercial Appeal*, "Little German Band to Give Benefit Concerts," April 28, 1927; *Commercial Appeal*, "To Aid Flood Sufferers," May 1, 1927; *Commercial Appeal*, "To Aid Flood Victims," April 29, 1927.

192. *Commercial Appeal*, "Response Is General to Pleas for Money," April 27, 1927; *Commercial Appeal*, "Relief Fund Nearing $100,000 Mark Here," May 4, 1927.

193. *Commercial Appeal*, "Telephone Company Contributes $25,000," May 6, 1927; *Commercial Appeal*, "Memphis K of C Give $1,000 to Flood Relief," May 8, 1927; *Commercial Appeal*, "Piggly Wiggly Check for $1,000 Received," May 10, 1927; *Commercial Appeal*, "Knights Templar Do Share, Send $1,000," May 27, 1927.

194. *Time*, "Flood Continued," May 16, 1927; William DeKleine, "Recent Health Observations in the Mississippi Flood Area," *American Journal of Public Health* 18, no. 2 (February 1, 1928): 146.

195. *Commercial Appeal*, "Epidemic Prevention Will Cost $1,000,000," May 18, 1927; *Memphis Evening Appeal*, "Health Chiefs Plan to Battle Refugees' Ills," April 26, 1927; *Commercial Appeal*, "Epidemic Prevention Will Cost $1,000,000," May 18, 1927.

196. *Commercial Appeal*, "Sanitation Problems Receive Attention," April 29, 1927; DeKleine, "Recent Health Observations in the Mississippi Flood Area," 147.

197. *New York Times*, "Disease Spreads in Wake of Floods," April 29, 1927; *Commercial Appeal*, "Sanitation Problems Receive Attention," April 29, 1927; *Commercial Appeal*, "Health Lines Taut in Flooded Section," May 5, 1927; *Commercial Appeal*, "Epidemic Prevention Will Cost $1,000,000," May 18, 1927.

198. *Commercial Appeal*, "Miami Loans Officer to Aid Flood Relief," May 15, 1927; *Commercial Appeal*, "Flood Area Health Will Be Discussed," May 22, 1927.

199. *New York Times*, "Donations Pour in for Relief," April 26, 1927; *Commercial Appeal*, "Six Health Officers Here from Baltimore," May 23, 1927; DeKleine, "Recent Health Observations in the Mississippi Flood Area," 147.

200. *Commercial Appeal*, "Malaria Expert Will Assist in Flood Area," May 22, 1927; DeKleine, "Recent Health Observations in the Mississippi Flood Area," 147–50.

201. Ibid.

202. DeKleine, "Recent Health Observations in the Mississippi Flood Area," 147–50; John Solomon Otto, *Final Frontiers, 1880–1930: Settling the Southern Bottomlands* (Westport, CT: Greenwood Press, 1999), 68.

203. *Commercial Appeal*, "Typhoid Clinics Will Help Present Health," April 27, 1927; *Commercial Appeal*, "Typhoid Treatments Will Be Given Free,"

April 28, 1927; *Commercial Appeal*, "Inoculate I.C. Workers," May 17, 1927; *Commercial Appeal*, "More Typhoid Clinics Will Be Inaugurated," May 29, 1927.

204. *Memphis Evening Appeal*, "Floods Threaten Memphis Highways," April 15, 1927; *Time*, "Water, Wind," April 25, 1927; *Commercial Appeal*, "Traffic Report," April 19, 1927.

205. *Memphis Evening Appeal*, "Memphis Prepares for Highest Water," April 18, 1927; *Memphis Evening Appeal*, "Vollentine Avenue People Flee Flood," April 15, 1927; *Memphis Evening Appeal*, "Fight to Save Memphis Mill Areas Grim," April 16, 1927; *Memphis Evening Appeal*, "Morning Rains; Chelsea Flood; Traffic Halted," April 20, 1927; *Memphis Evening Appeal*, "Woman, Bedridden, Saved from Flood," April 20, 1927.

206. *Memphis Evening Appeal*, "Fight to Save Memphis Mill Areas Grim," April 16, 1927; *Memphis Evening Appeal*, "Shelby Highways Covered by Floods," April 16, 1927; *Commercial Appeal*, Highway No. 1 Closed," April 21, 1927; *Memphis Evening Appeal*, "Bridge Goes Out; Road to South Cut," April 23, 1927; *Memphis Evening Appeal*, "Heavy Rains in Shelby Damage Graveled Roads," April 20, 1927.

207. *Memphis Evening Appeal*, "Fight to Save Memphis Mill Areas Grim," April 16, 1927; *Memphis Evening Appeal*, "Flood Menaces Horn Lake Road: To Stop Travel," April 15, 1927; *Memphis Evening Appeal*, "Shelby Highways Covered by Floods," April 16, 1927; *Memphis Evening Appeal*, "Bridge Goes Out; Road to South Cut," April 23, 1927.

208. Ibid.

209. *Memphis Evening Appeal*, "Flood Menaces Horn Lake Road: To Stop Travel," April 15, 1927; *Memphis Evening Appeal*, "Fight to Save Memphis Mill Areas Grim," April 16, 1927; *Memphis Evening Appeal*, "Memphis Prepares for Highest Water," April 18, 1927.

210. *Commercial Appeal*, "All Shelby Roads Are Now Open to Travel," April 29, 1927; *Commercial Appeal*, "Jefferson Covered with Bayou Waters," May 10, 1927.

211. *Memphis Evening Appeal*, "Fight to Save Memphis Mill Areas Grim," April 16, 1927; *Commercial Appeal*, "Lightning Hits St. Mary's Cathedral; Organ Damaged," April 21, 1927.

212. *Commercial Appeal*, "Riverbank Control Plans to Be Formed," May 27, 1927.

213. *Commercial Appeal*, "Industrial Growth of Memphis Sought," April 21, 1927.

214. *Commercial Appeal*, "Libeling Memphis," May 6, 1927; *Commercial Appeal*, "Rail, River Routes Give Memphis Favor," May 14, 1927.

215. Letter from Paine to President of Kiwanis, May 21, 1927, Rowlett Paine Collection, Box 13.

216. Daniel, *Deep'n as It Come*, 72–73; Risk Management Solutions, Inc., *The 1927 Great Mississippi Flood*, 6.

217. *Commercial Appeal*, "Elaborate Organization Set Up to Aid Stricken Section," May 3, 1927.

218. *Commercial Appeal*, "Refugee Women Busy Learning Home Needs," May 10, 1927; *Commercial Appeal*, "Elaborate Organization Set Up to Aid Stricken Section," May 3, 1927; *Commercial Appeal*, "Miami Loans Officer to Aid Flood Relief," May 15, 1927.

219. *Commercial Appeal*, "Red Cross Moves Its Base to New Orleans," May 26, 1927.

220. *Commercial Appeal*, "Co-Op Club to Hear Story of the Flood," May 18, 1927; *Commercial Appeal*, "Kilpatrick Directs Rehabilitation Work," May 27, 1927.

221. *Commercial Appeal*, "Cloudbursts Add to Misery from Floods," May 7, 1927; *Commercial Appeal*, "Dozens of Towns Struck in Path of Tornado Over MO, Arkansas," May 10, 1927; *Commercial Appeal*, "Poplar Bluff Rent by Worst Tornado in History of Missouri," May 11, 1927; *Commercial Appeal*, "Need Larger Relief Fund for Refugees," May 12, 1927.

222. *Commercial Appeal*, "New Madrid Fault Caused Earthquake," May 8, 1927; Springer, *Nobody Knows Where the Blues Came From*, 9.

223. *Time*, "Flood Continued," May 16, 1927; *Memphis Evening Appeal*, "Dyke Goes Out at South Bend; Adds to Flood," April 25, 1927.

224. *Memphis Evening Appeal*, "Red Cross Chapter Here Keeping Busy," April 26, 1927.

225. *Commercial Appeal*, "Walton League Saves Wild Life from Flood," May 4, 1927; *Memphis Evening Appeal*, "Memphis Heeds Cry for Boats and Provisions," April 23, 1927;

226. *Time*, "Water, Wind," April 25, 1927; *New York Times*, "Snakes Menace Refugees," April 25, 1927.

227. *New York Times*, "Red Cross Is Succoring 80,000 Destitute as Flood Spreads Over 9,000 Square Miles; Property Loss May Reach $1,000,000," April 25, 1927; *Commercial Appeal*, "Floods in the South Save Mills in the North," May 30, 1927.

228. *New York Times*, "Cotton Crop Hit by South's Flood," April 26, 1927.

229. *Commercial Appeal*, "150,000 Bales Damaged," May 3, 1927; *Commercial Appeal*, "Overproduction of Cotton Yet Menaces," May 24, 1927.

230. *Memphis Evening Appeal*, "Arkansas Still Seized," April 19, 1927; *Time*, "Flood Continued," May 16, 1927.

231. Clay, *A Century on the Mississippi*, 94; *Commercial Appeal*, "Will Repair Levees to Beat June Flood," May 17, 1927; *Commercial Appeal*, "Star Levee Work," May 27, 1927; Barry, *Rising Tide*, 285.

232. *Commercial Appeal*, "War Preparedness Was Godsend During Flood," May 17, 1927.

233. *Memphis Evening Appeal*, "Lesson from the Flood," April 25, 1927.

Chapter 7

234. *Time*, "Flood Continued," May 16, 1927.

235. Pearcy, "After the Flood," 176; Bukowski, *Big Bill Thompson*, 191.

236. Pearcy, "After the Flood," 177.

237. *Commercial Appeal*, "Coolidge Will Send Engineers to South," May 4, 1927.

238. Pearcy, "After the Flood," 177; *Commercial Appeal*, "Congressional Party to View Flood Area," May 2, 1927; *New York Times*, "House Committeemen Will Visit Stricken Zone," April 26, 1927; *Commercial Appeal*, "Senators' Flood Itinerary Made Up," May 17, 1927.

239. *Commercial Appeal*, "Connolly on River Tour," May 29, 1927; *Commercial Appeal*, "Congressmen Seeing Arkansas Flood Area," May 31, 1927.

240. Letter from Paine to Luke Lea, June 7, 1927, Rowlett Paine Collection, Box 13.

241. *Commercial Appeal*, "20,000 Expected at Chicago Conference," May 31, 1927; *Time*, "Oratory," June 13, 1927.

242. *Time*, "Oratory," June 13, 1927.

243. Ibid.

244. *New York Times*, "Urge Coolidge Call for Parley," June 5, 1927; *Time*, "Oratory," June 13, 1927.

245. *New York Times*, "Urge Coolidge Call for Parley," June 5, 1927; Bukowski, *Big Bill Thompson*, 192; Pearcy, "After the Flood," 177.

246. Pearcy, "After the Flood," 178.

247. Ibid., 177.

248. Ibid., 182–83.

249. Ibid.

250. Ibid., 184.

251. Ibid., 183–90.

252. Capers, *Mississippi River*, 1–2.

253. Robert Sigafoos, *Cotton Row to Beale Street: A Business History of Memphis* (Memphis: Memphis State University Press, 1979), 140.

254. Paine sends regrets about not attending various meetings, July–October 1927, Rowlett Paine Collection, Box 13.

255. G. Wayne Dowdy, *Mayor Crump Don't Like It: Machine Politics in Memphis* (Oxford: University Press of Mississippi, 2006), 45–53.

256. Ibid.

257. Sharon D. Wright, *Race, Power, and Political Emergence in Memphis* (New York: Routledge, 1999), 36.
258. Dowdy, *Mayor Crump Don't Like It*, 45–53.

EPILOGUE

259. Memphis Minnie, *Queen of the Blues*.
260. *New York Times*, "Hoover's Own Picture of the Flood Tragedy," May 22, 1927.
261. Dowdy, *Mayor Crump Don't Like It*, 62.

INDEX

A

African Americans 9, 30, 31, 32, 35,
    36, 58, 73, 115
aircraft 50, 63, 64, 66, 72, 82
Akers, Larry S. 60
Alcorn, DeWitt T. 45
Allen, D.G. (Mrs.) 39
Allen, Thomas 87
American Legion 40, 44, 61, 77
Anderson, C.M. 69
Andreucetti, Ulbaldo 62
animals 21, 39, 103, 104, 105
Arkansas 7, 8, 12, 13, 15, 16, 17, 18, 19,
    20, 21, 22, 24, 25, 26, 34, 35, 36,
    40, 41, 43, 46, 47, 49, 50, 52, 55,
    56, 57, 59, 61, 62, 63, 66, 70, 72,
    74, 76, 79, 80, 81, 90, 91, 101,
    102, 103, 104, 109, 112
Arkansas City, Arkansas 21, 24
Arkansas River 22
Augustine, steamer 25, 54

B

Bailey, H.W. 26
Baker, Henry M. 26, 52, 53, 54, 55,
    64, 67, 68, 69, 70, 71, 72, 73,
    83, 87, 89, 90, 102, 107

Barbour, Jeptha Fowlkes 32
Barnesworth, M.C. 26
Barron, John 66
Barron, William E. 17
Barry, John 36
Bates, Bert 41
Bayless, W.B. 41, 50, 83
Beachley, R.G. (Dr.) 90
Beale Street 106
Bedford, W.H. 41
Bellomini, John 114
Beneke, Fred D. 109
Benjestown Road 95
Big Creek 95
Big Creek Bridge 95
Binswanger, Milton S. 100
Black Fish Bayou, Arkansas 50
Blackwood, Dwight H. 25
Blytheville, Arkansas 26, 89
Bonslagle, Connie 101, 102
bootleggers 106
Boy Scouts 87
Briark, Arkansas 41
Brickeys, Arkansas 25
Brist, Frederick W. 15, 16, 17
Brown, Reese 58
Brown, S.W. (Dr.) 45
Bruce, C. Arthur 79

Bry's Department Store 65
Burke's Landing, Mississippi 16
Burleson, Raymond 58

C

Caernarvon, Louisiana 101
Cairo, Illinois 11, 12, 13, 15, 16, 17, 18, 70
Campbell, J.L. (Reverend) 45
Canale, Jim 55, 56
Cape Girardeau, steamer 11, 12, 16, 59
Caraway, T.H. 74
Carley, Jack 41, 43
Carmichael, B.B. 33
Carpenter, A.B. 41
Carter, Winston 55
Cat Island, Mississippi 56
Catledge, Turner 70, 73, 74
Cayuga, towboat 53
chamber of commerce 32, 68, 70, 75, 79, 80, 100, 106
Chappell, Clovis G. 88
Chicago, Illinois 11, 12, 26, 34, 35, 62, 77, 86, 100, 109, 110, 111, 114
Chiozza, Mario 62
Chisca Hotel 78
Chisca, steamer 58
Choctaw, steamer 17, 50, 52, 54
Choctaw Transportation Service 17
Church, Robert, Jr. 115
Cincinnati, steamer 11, 12, 53
City Club 114
Clarendon, Arkansas 17, 19, 20, 109
Clark, Ernest 29
Cleveland, Mississippi 29, 30, 55, 74
Colby, Henry R. 55
Colored Advisory Commission 35, 36
Columbian Mutual Life Insurance 85
Colwell, Helen 26
Commercial Appeal 16, 33, 37, 52, 55, 58, 63, 70, 72, 75, 85, 88
Connolly, Donald H. 15, 16, 17, 41, 51, 52, 64, 66, 100, 106, 109

Coolidge, Calvin 8, 9, 30, 68, 77, 78, 81, 83, 85, 109, 110, 111, 112, 113
Cooper, Henry 58
Cortese Brothers' East End Garden 87
Cotton Exchange 105
Cotton Plant, Arkansas 24, 25
cotton production 105
Couch, Harvey 75
Cox, Charles 41
Craig, Charles 58
Craig, Oscar 58
Crittenden County, Arkansas 25, 46
Crosby, L.O. 32, 79
Crowley's Ridge, Arkansas 22, 25
Crump, Edward H. 45, 114, 115
Cummins, Hugh S. 90

D

dams 17, 22, 95
Daniel, Pete 34
Davant, James 100
Davis, Dwight 8, 30, 72, 109, 110, 111
Dawes, Charles 61
del Prete, Carlo 62
DeMond, A.L. (Reverend) 45
de Pinedo, Francesco 62
DeSomoskeoy, B.H. (Dr.) 90
DeVall's Bluff, Arkansas 17
Di Gaetani, John 62
Doe, C.P. 101
Dorena, Missouri 106, 109
Douglas, Pearl 58
Doull, James A. (Dr.) 90
Durrett, J.J. (Dr.) 41
dysentery 21

E

Eads Colored School 91
earthquakes 103
Elliott, V.L. (Dr.) 90
Ellis Auditorium 41, 44, 46, 86, 87
Ellithorp, Frank 68
Elmwood Cemetery 58
Emmerson, Louis 12

Evening Appeal 29, 30, 52, 55, 58, 63, 74, 85, 87, 89

F

Fant, A.P. 100
Federal Intermediate Credit Corporation 78
Field, R.S. (Dr.) 89
Fieser, James L. 35, 36, 39, 68, 69, 71, 72, 102, 107
Fifteen Mile Bayou, Arkansas 40
Flood Control Act of 1928 9
flood stage, record set 97
Flournoy, Frank 52
Flowers, Hays 80
Ford auto plant 101
Fordyce, John R. 75
Forrest City, Arkansas 20, 24, 25, 26, 50, 52, 102, 104
Fowler, William 97, 100
Fox, Elizabeth 90
Franconi, John L. 87
Fuller, T.O. 45

G

Galella, John 62
Gaston, Jesse 41
Gay, Hubert 66
Gayoso Hotel 78, 87
Gellespie, Harold 49
George J. James School 91
Giesen, Mary Barrow 101
Goldberger, Jospeh (Dr.) 91
Good Friday storm 17, 22
Graham-Merrin Company 86
Graves, L.M. (Dr.) 91
Greenbriar, boat 53
Green, Phil 40
Greenville, Mississippi 17, 18, 29, 31, 32, 33, 41, 52, 54, 55, 56, 59, 61, 64, 69, 70, 71, 73, 74, 89, 103, 105, 109
Gregory, Joe 67

Grubbs, D.C.T. 52
Guyandot, steamer 53, 54

H

Harahan Bridge 7, 43, 46
hardwood industry 105, 114
Hardy, Arkansas 22
Harry Lee, steamer 25
Harvey, Malinde 90
Hayden, Frank 79
Helena, Arkansas 24, 26, 54, 55, 58, 61
Henderson, Jospeh H. 58
Henry, Charles 58
Heth, Arkansas 40
Hickman, Kentucky 12, 15, 17, 46
Hicks, Clara 58
highways 17, 24, 25
Hindman Ferry Road 95
Hollywood neighborhood 94
Hooper, Joe 49
Hoover, Herbert 8, 9, 35, 36, 37, 46, 65, 68, 69, 70, 71, 72, 73, 74, 75, 76, 77, 78, 79, 80, 81, 87, 91, 101, 107, 109, 110, 115, 117, 118
Horn Lake Road 96, 99
Hotel Sherman 110
Huffstetter, C.E. 28
Hugo, Robert 41
Hunter, Chatham and Manuel 66
Hutchinson, Ed 49

I

Illinois 8, 11, 12, 13, 15, 16, 17, 18, 70, 73, 76, 92, 97, 99, 100, 101, 102, 103, 109, 111
Interstate Commerce Commission 61
Interstate Seed Crushers Association 78
Iroquois, towboat 53
Izaak Walton League 104

J

Jackson, Sam 49
Jadwin, Edwin 46, 51, 68, 71, 76, 77, 101, 106, 107, 110, 112, 113
John Barrett, steamer 53, 54
Johnson, Jean 87
Johnson, J.M. 79
Jones, Luther F. 95
Jones, Paul 41
Jones-Reid Bill 113
Jones, Sam 61
Joy, Melville 41

K

Kankakee, steamer 54, 55
Kennedy Dry Dock 106
Kennett, Missouri 17
Kennington, R.E. 79
Kentucky 8, 12, 13, 15, 16, 17, 18, 27, 46, 52, 66, 70, 76, 101, 102, 103
Kerrville School 92
Kilpatrick, Earl 67, 102
King, W.R. 79
Kiwanis Club 101
Knowlton's Point, Arkansas 57

L

labor agents 32
Laconia Circle, Arkansas 16, 106
LaFollette, Robert 78
Lake City, Arkansas 17
Larry, Susie 38
Lea, Luke 110
Lee, George W. 115
Leftwich, Frank 49
Leland, Mississippi 33
LePrince, Jospeh A. (Dr.) 90, 91
Leroy, Louis (Dr.) 55, 56, 73, 88
Lester, Arkansas 17
levees 7, 8, 12, 13, 15, 16, 21, 22, 27, 29, 31, 34, 35, 36, 39, 44, 46, 51, 54, 55, 64, 76, 78, 81, 97, 104, 106, 110, 111, 112, 118
Lick Creek 92

Light, Harry 41
Lindbergh, Charles 82
Little River 17, 24
Little Rock, Arkansas 13, 17, 21, 24, 26, 60, 62, 66, 75, 80, 100
loans to farmers 79
Loew's Palace Theater 87, 88
Loew's Theater 86, 87, 88
Loosahatchie River 95
Louisiana 8, 15, 21, 35, 46, 52, 53, 76, 79, 80, 101, 102, 108
Lucy School 92
Lumsden, L.L. (Dr.) 90
Lutz, J.C. 80
Lyceum Theater 86

M

malaria 21, 22, 89, 90, 91
Marked Tree, Arkansas 17, 22, 24, 26, 109
Mark Twain, boat 56
Martineau, John 74, 75
Martin, J.B. (Dr.) 115
Mary Frances, steamer 49, 50, 52
McCall, John E. 41
McClelland, Arkansas 24
McDowell, J.D. 79
McLain, Tyler 114
McLaughlin, Allen (Dr.) 90
McMullen, John (Dr.) 90, 91
measles 90
Mellon, Andrew 8, 53
Mellwood, Arkansas 18, 24
Memphis 7, 9, 12, 13, 15, 16, 17, 18, 19, 25, 26, 29, 30, 31, 32, 34, 35, 37, 38, 40, 41, 43, 44, 45, 46, 47, 48, 49, 50, 51, 52, 54, 55, 57, 58, 59, 61, 62, 63, 64, 65, 66, 67, 68, 70, 72, 73, 74, 75, 76, 77, 78, 79, 80, 81, 82, 83, 85, 87, 88, 89, 90, 91, 92, 94, 95, 100, 101, 102, 103, 104, 105, 106, 109, 113, 114, 115, 117, 118
Memphis Garden Club 87

Memphis Junior League 86, 87
Memphis Rehabilitation Committee 80
Memphis Street Railway 87
Mercury, steamer 50
Messick School 92
Michael, Henry 49
Mid-South 9, 15, 16, 17, 18, 45, 46, 48, 49, 63, 64, 65, 67, 76, 77, 102, 105, 114, 118
Millington 91, 95
Millington Central High School 91
Millington Colored School 92
Mississippi 7, 8, 9, 11, 12, 13, 15, 16, 17, 18, 21, 22, 25, 28, 29, 30, 32, 35, 39, 46, 47, 49, 52, 53, 55, 56, 57, 58, 59, 61, 62, 63, 66, 67, 68, 69, 70, 71, 72, 73, 74, 75, 76, 77, 79, 80, 81, 82, 83, 86, 89, 90, 92, 94, 96, 100, 101, 102, 103, 104, 105, 106, 107, 108, 109, 110, 111, 112, 113, 114, 117, 118
Mississippi Rehabilitation Corporation 79, 80
Mississippi River 7, 8, 11, 12, 13, 15, 17, 21, 22, 46, 49, 57, 62, 70, 72, 75, 76, 81, 92, 94, 100, 106, 108, 109, 111, 113, 118
Mississippi Valley Flood Control Association 109
Missouri 8, 9, 13, 17, 18, 20, 22, 25, 41, 52, 59, 61, 67, 78, 101, 102, 103, 109, 113
Mitchell, P.A. 26
Moreland, George 33
Morris, C.L. 58
Morris, W.B. 58
mosquitoes 21
Moton, Robert R. 35
movies 11, 87, 88
mules 21, 34, 38, 46
mumps 90
Murphree, Dennis Herron 30, 32, 72, 73

N

National Guard 20, 32, 35, 36
Navaho, boat 56
navy yard levee 97
Neal, Ernest 58
New Madrid, Missouri 18, 24, 59, 109, 113
New Orleans, Louisiana 11, 17, 51, 54, 61, 64, 67, 71, 73, 74, 76, 77, 101, 102, 108, 110, 113
Newsum, Thornton 55
Nineteenth Century Club 87
Nonconnah Creek 92, 95
Norfleet, J.P. 79
North Memphis Civic Improvement Club 88
North Second Street Bridge 95
Noyes, Clara D. 90
nurses 90

O

Ohio River 15, 53
Ohio Valley 17
O'Keefe, Arthur 11, 108, 110, 111
Oleando, steamer 53
Omilie, Vernon and Phoebe 62, 66
Ottawa, towboat 53
Overton, Watkins 115
Owen, H.N. 58
Owens, S.A. (Reverend) 45

P

Paducah, Mississippi 29
Paine, Elizabeth "Sugar" 82
Paine, Rowlett 13, 31, 40, 41, 42, 62, 68, 69, 70, 82, 83, 87, 95, 100, 101, 109, 110, 111, 114, 115, 118
Pantages Theater 86, 88
Parkin, William 50
Patricia Barrett, steamer 53
Patterson, L.G. (Dr.) 45
Pawnee, steamer 53
Peabody Hotel 25, 59, 66, 69, 70, 86, 88

Peay, Austin 88
Pelican, launch 57, 58
Percy, Leroy 74
Percy, Will 74
Pine Bluff, Arkansas 22, 24, 25, 26, 62
Plough Chemical Company 80
police 7, 11, 17, 32, 35, 41, 43, 47, 70, 87, 99, 114, 115
Polk, C.W. (Dr.) 91
Poplar Bluff, Missouri 22, 102
Preston, E.L. 26
Prohibition agents 106

R

radio 45, 50, 51, 52, 53, 76, 77, 88
Ragland, S.E. 79
railroads 17, 20, 25, 29, 41, 59, 61, 73, 78, 92, 97, 100, 109
Ramsey, A.D. 106
Raney, William 43
Rapp, William C. 41
Rawlinson, Arkansas 50
Red Cross 8, 18, 25, 26, 30, 31, 32, 35, 38, 39, 40, 41, 43, 44, 45, 46, 50, 52, 55, 58, 61, 64, 66, 67, 68, 69, 70, 72, 74, 76, 77, 78, 79, 80, 82, 83, 85, 86, 87, 88, 89, 90, 91, 101, 102, 104, 107, 118
Redden, William R. (Dr.) 89, 90, 91, 103
Redmond, Sidney Dillon 36
Reelfoot Lake 15, 28
refugee camps 8, 18, 21, 25, 26, 32, 35, 36, 37, 40, 41, 45, 46, 52, 55, 56, 58, 61, 70, 73, 74, 79, 89, 90, 101, 104
refugees 7, 9, 12, 13, 18, 25, 26, 30, 32, 34, 35, 37, 38, 39, 40, 41, 43, 44, 45, 46, 47, 49, 50, 52, 54, 55, 56, 61, 64, 69, 70, 74, 78, 85, 89, 91, 100, 101, 102, 104, 105, 117, 118
Reichman-Crosby Company 80
Reid, Frank 109, 111
Remmer, H.L. 78

Rhea, W.P. 41
Rugby Park Road 95

S

sabotage of levees 28
Saloman, Ed 65
Salon Circle, civic organization 88
Salvation Army 40
Santa Maria II, airplane 62
Sawner, Thomas Edward 58
schools 41, 45, 90, 91, 92
Schultz, Claude 41
Scott's Landing, Mississippi 28, 29, 30, 55, 103
Sears and Roebuck 83
sharecroppers 34, 35, 36, 40, 79
Shawnee, steamer 53
Shelby County Anti-Tuberculosis Society 91
Shelby County Colored Training School 92
smallpox 89, 90, 91
Smith, Al 83
Smith, Frank 49
Smith, H.B. 41
Snowden, Robert 79, 80, 81
Spalding, George R. 31, 52, 53, 54, 70, 73, 106
Spencer, Robyn 34
Spurling, W.B. 41
Sterling, Fred E. 12
St. Francis River 15, 21, 22, 24, 26, 49, 50, 52, 60, 61
St. Joseph's Hospital 94
St. Mary's Cathedral 99
Stone, W.C. (Dr.) 90
Stratton, L.M. 80
Sullivan, Eddie J. 86
Sunday Movie Bill 88
Sunshine, boat 56

T

Tallapoosa, steamer 53
telegraph service 17, 25, 52, 53

telephones 17, 19, 25, 43, 51, 52, 53, 55, 73, 76, 99

Tennessee 8, 13, 15, 18, 27, 41, 46, 52, 55, 76, 79, 87, 88, 101, 102, 103, 110, 115

theaters 86, 87, 88

Thomas, D.J. (Dr.) 45

Thompson, William Hale 11, 12, 13, 108, 109, 110, 111, 113

Tiptonville, Tennessee 15

tornadoes 39, 56, 102

Treadwell School 92

Trent, Walter 42

Tri-State Fairgrounds 18, 38, 39, 40, 42, 43, 44, 45, 46, 47, 69, 70, 86, 104, 118

Tri-State Flood Control Committee 112

Trumann, Arkansas 22, 24

Tucker, Sam 57

Tulot, Arkansas 22

Turner, Renfro 25, 29, 40, 46

Tuscombia, steamer 53

Tutwiler Street 92

Tutwiler, T.H. 80

typhoid 21, 30, 64, 85, 89, 90, 91

U

United States Army 15, 42, 44, 51, 52, 72, 89, 111, 112

United States Coast Guard 53, 54

United States Navy 62, 72, 83, 90

University of Arkansas Extension Department 78

U.S. Army Corps of Engineers 12, 15, 18, 31, 41, 46, 50, 51, 52, 53, 58, 59, 66, 68, 73, 76, 100, 106, 109, 112, 113

USS *Memphis*, light cruiser 82

V

Vallery, J.A. (Dr.) 92

Van Vleet Mansfield Drug Company 85

Vicksburg, Mississippi 15, 30, 31, 46, 54, 61, 64, 66, 71, 73, 74, 83, 102

Vollintine Street 92

W

Wabash, steamer 15, 54, 57, 74, 105

Waddell, John 41

Wake Robin, boat 53

Walden, Carol 49

Walker, Johnson 106

Waring, Roane 41, 43, 44, 45, 62

Weather Bureau 8, 15, 18

Weatherby, F.C. 40

West, Wally 32

Whitehall, Arkansas 25, 40, 49, 106

White, John 58

White, Walter 36

Whittington, William 75

Widener, Arkansas 49

Wilbur, Curtis 8

Wilcox, Paul C. 102

Wilkerson, Wayman 115

Williams, K.G. 100

WMC radio station 52, 70, 75, 100

Wolf River 92, 95

Wright, Richard 34

Y

Yandel, Marshall 41

Yazoo County, Mississippi 29, 31, 32, 54, 74, 103

YMCA 49, 88

York, Mark 69

Z

Zacchetti, Vitale 62

ABOUT THE AUTHOR

Patrick O'Daniel is a professional librarian in Memphis, Tennessee. He worked for the Memphis Public Library and Information Center for over sixteen years, spending nine years in the history/social sciences department working with archival and genealogical collections. He has a master's degree in history from the University of Memphis and a master's degree in information sciences from the University of Tennessee, Knoxville. He also studied at the Institute of Genealogy and Historical Research at Samford University in Birmingham, Alabama. Patrick lives in Memphis with his wife, Kathy, and daughter, Kelly.